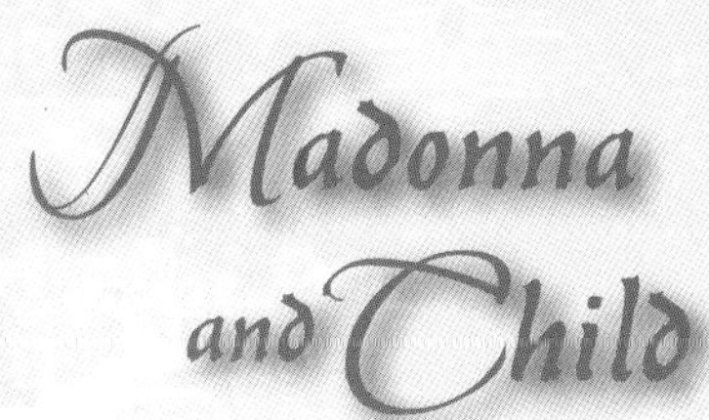

Madonna and Child

The State Hermitage Museum, St. Petersburg

arca publishers

Pomegranate
SAN FRANCISCO

A BOOK OF POSTCARDS

Pomegranate Communications, Inc.
Box 808022, Petaluma CA 94975
800 227 1428; www.pomegranate.com

Pomegranate Europe Ltd.
Unit 1, Heathcote Business Centre, Hurlbutt Road
Warwick, Warwickshire CV34 6TD, UK
[+44] 0 1926 430111; sales@pomeurope.co.uk

ISBN 978-0-7649-4405-5
Pomegranate Catalog No. AA428

Pomegranate publishes books of postcards on a wide range of subjects.
Please contact the publisher for more information.

Cover designed by Lora Santiago
Printed in Korea
16 15 14 13 12 11 10 09 08 10 9 8 7 6 5 4 3 2

To facilitate detachment of the postcards from this book, fold each card along its perforation line before tearing.

The State Hermitage Museum, in the heart of historic St. Petersburg, occupies an ensemble of magnificent buildings on the bank of the River Neva. The grandest of all is the Winter Palace—the former residence of the Russian czars—designed by Francesco Bartolomeo Rastrelli and constructed from 1754 to 1762. Within the walls of this artistic enclave reside the Hermitage collections, about three million works that trace the development of world art and culture from the Stone Age to today. The museum is currently enhancing its digital self-portrait to provide people around the world with wider access to information about its remarkable treasures.

Selected from this monumental trove are the thirty paintings featured in this book of postcards. The renowned collections of the State Hermitage Museum (and this book) include works by Raphael, Leonardo da Vinci, Palma il Vecchio, Jan Provost, Joos van Cleve, and many other worldwide favorites.

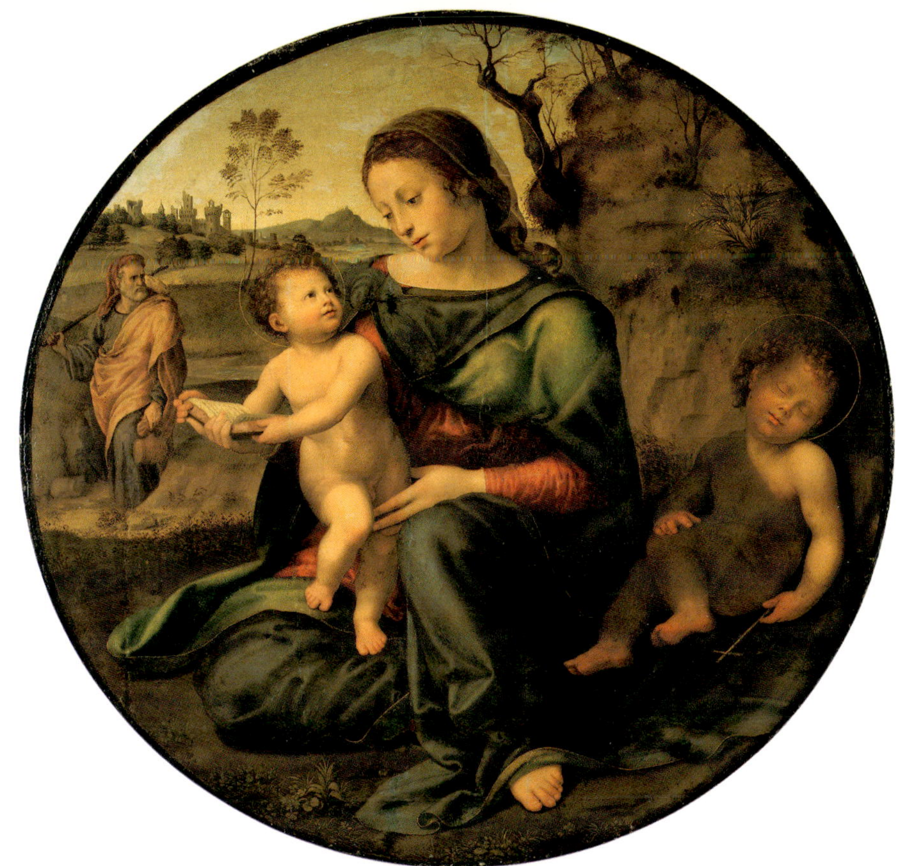

Madonna and Child

Giulio Bugiardini (Italian, 1475–1554)
The Holy Family with St. John the Baptist, c. 1520
Oil on canvas (transferred from panel),
89 cm (35 1⁄16 in.) diameter
The State Hermitage Museum, St. Petersburg

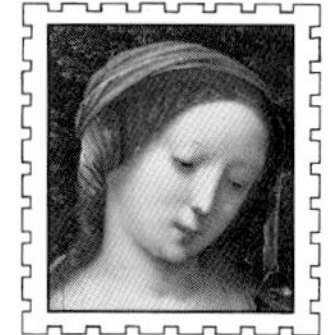

Pomegranate 707 782 9000 WWW.POMEGRANATE.COM

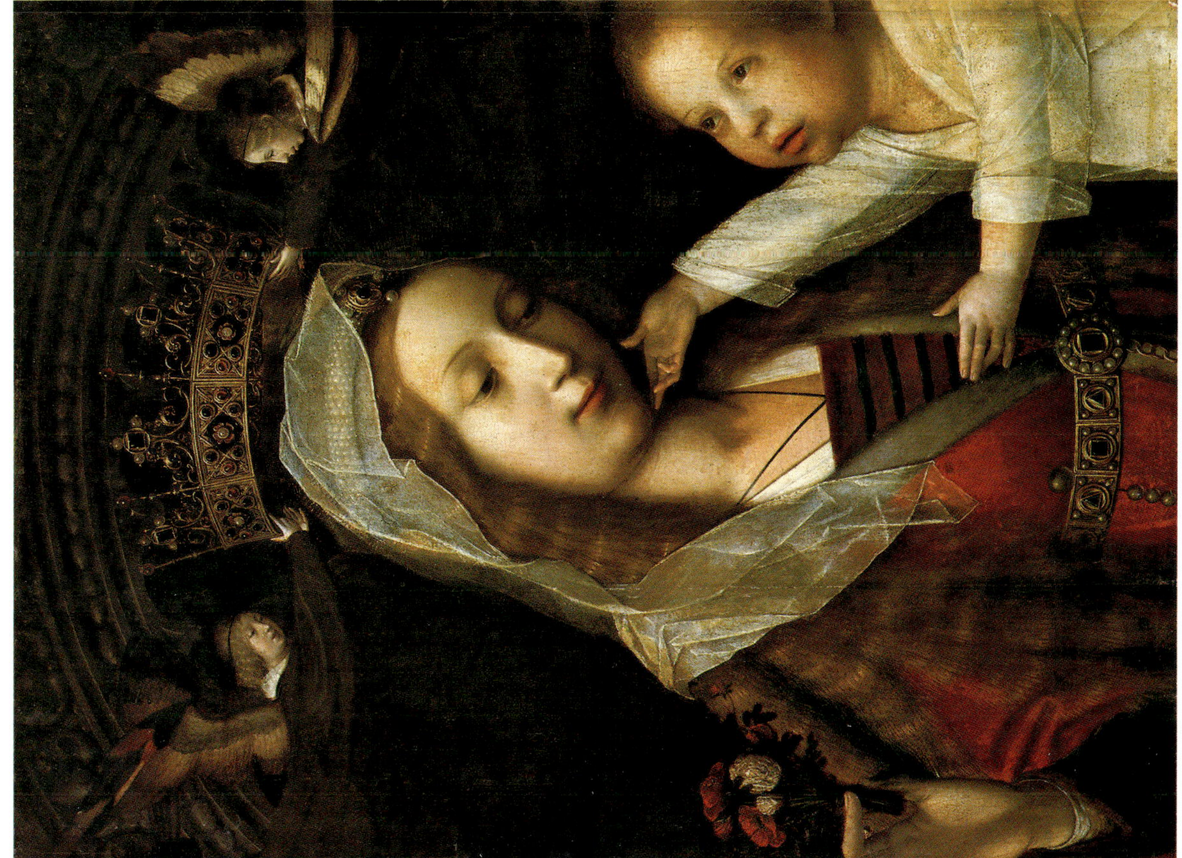

Madonna and Child

Jan Provost (Netherlandish, c. 1465–1529)
The Virgin and Child, n.d.
Oil on panel, 63.5 x 47 cm (25 x 18½ in.)
The State Hermitage Museum, St. Petersburg

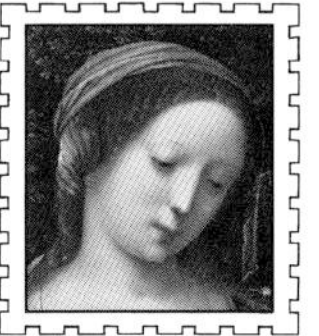

Pomegranate 707 782 9000 WWW.POMEGRANATE.COM

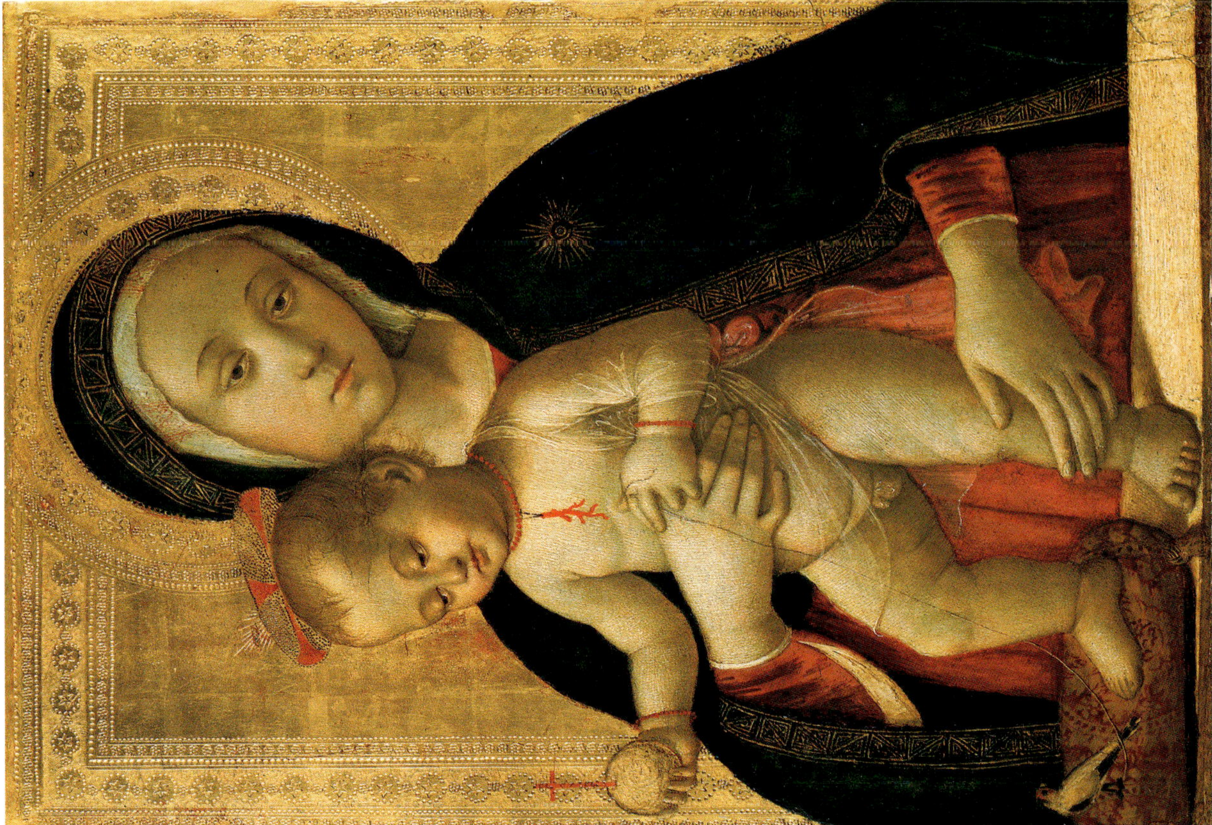

Madonna and Child

Bernardino Fungai (Italian, 1460–1516)
Madonna and Child, fifteenth century
Tempera on panel, 47 x 34 cm (18½ x 13⅜ in.)
The State Hermitage Museum, St. Petersburg

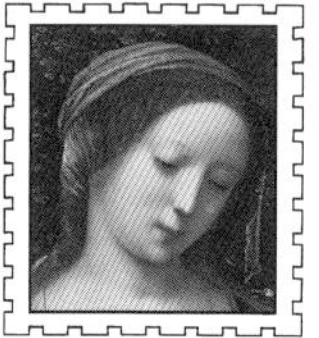

Pomegranate 707 782 9000 WWW.POMEGRANATE.COM

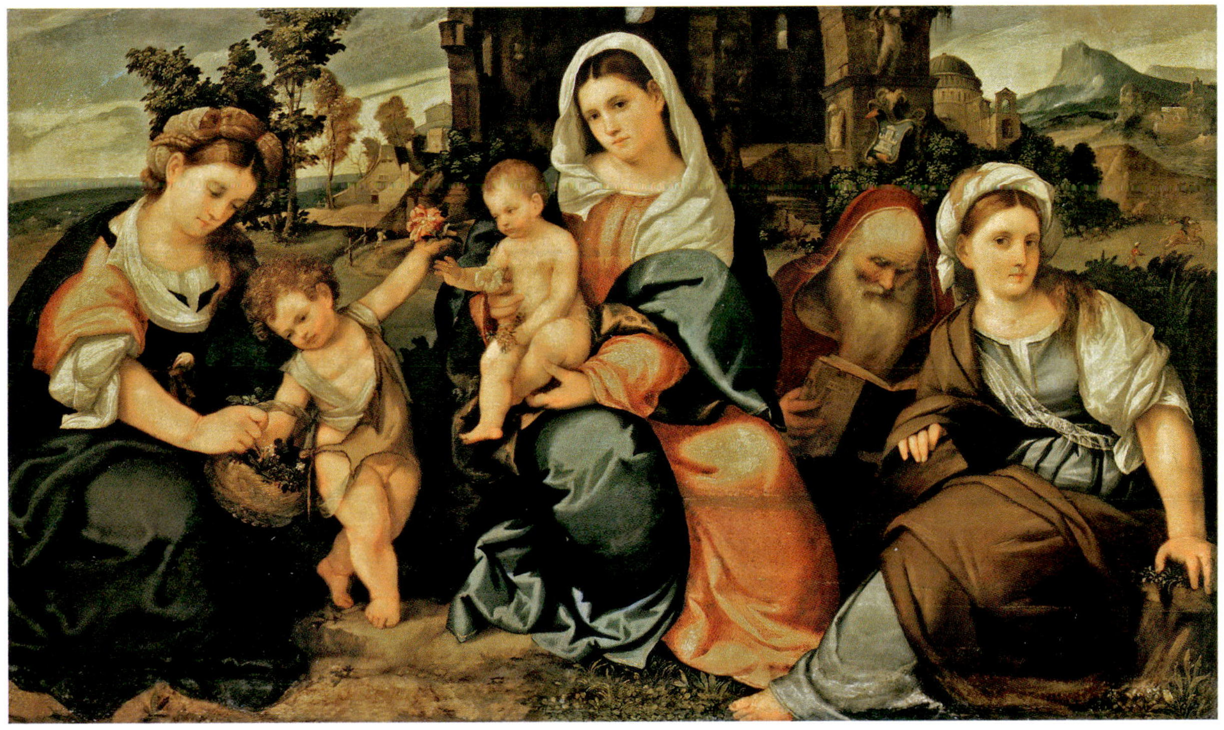

Madonna and Child

Bonifazio Veronese (Bonifazio di Pitati) (Italian, 1487–1553)
Madonna and Child with Saints Catherine, John the Baptist, Dorothy and Jerome, 1523–1525
Oil on canvas (transferred from panel),
80 x 135 cm (31½ x 53⅛ in.)
The State Hermitage Museum, St. Petersburg

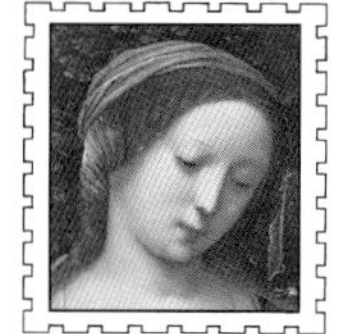

Pomegranate 707 782 9000 WWW.POMEGRANATE.COM

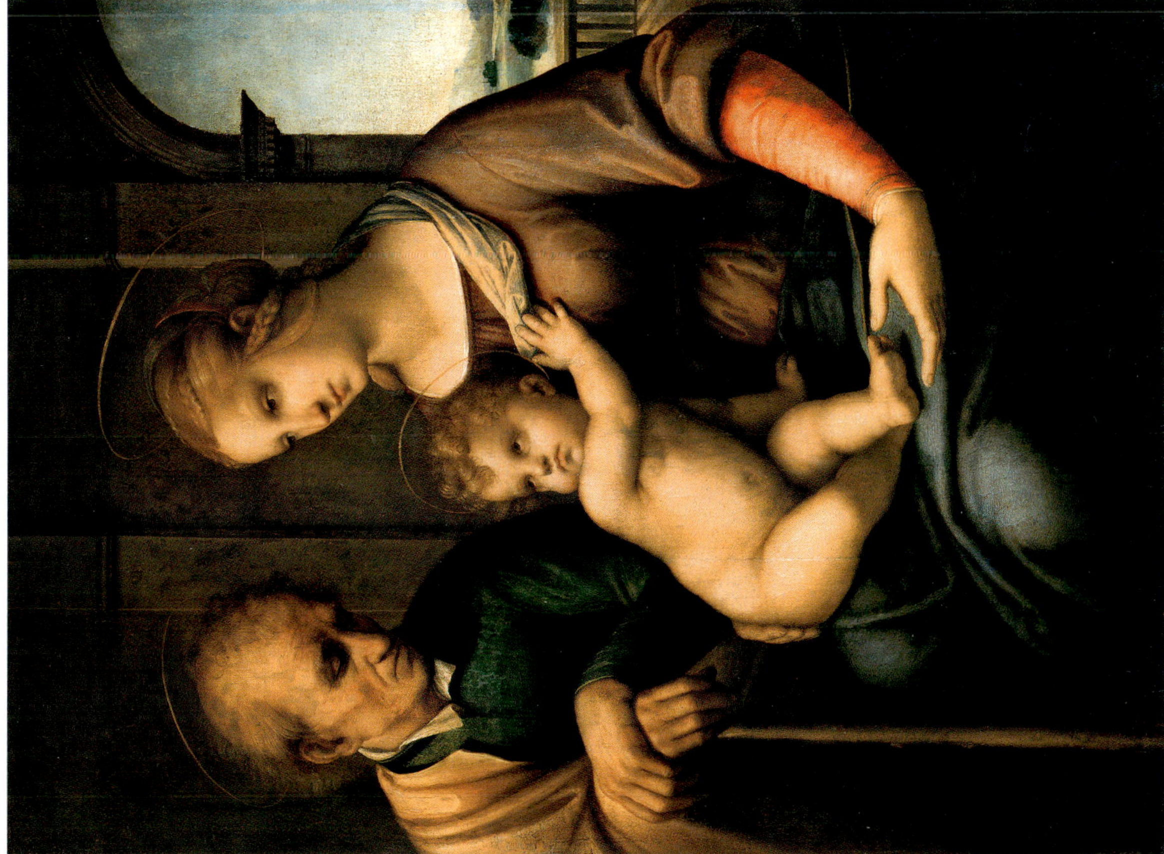

Madonna and Child

Raphael (Raffaello Santi or Sanzio) (Italian, 1483–1520)
The Holy Family (Madonna with the Beardless Joseph),
1505–1506
Tempera and oil on canvas (transferred from panel),
72.5 x 56.5 cm (28 9/16 x 22¼ in.)
The State Hermitage Museum, St. Petersburg

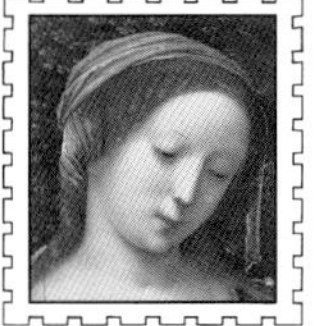

Pomegranate 707 782 9000 WWW.POMEGRANATE.COM

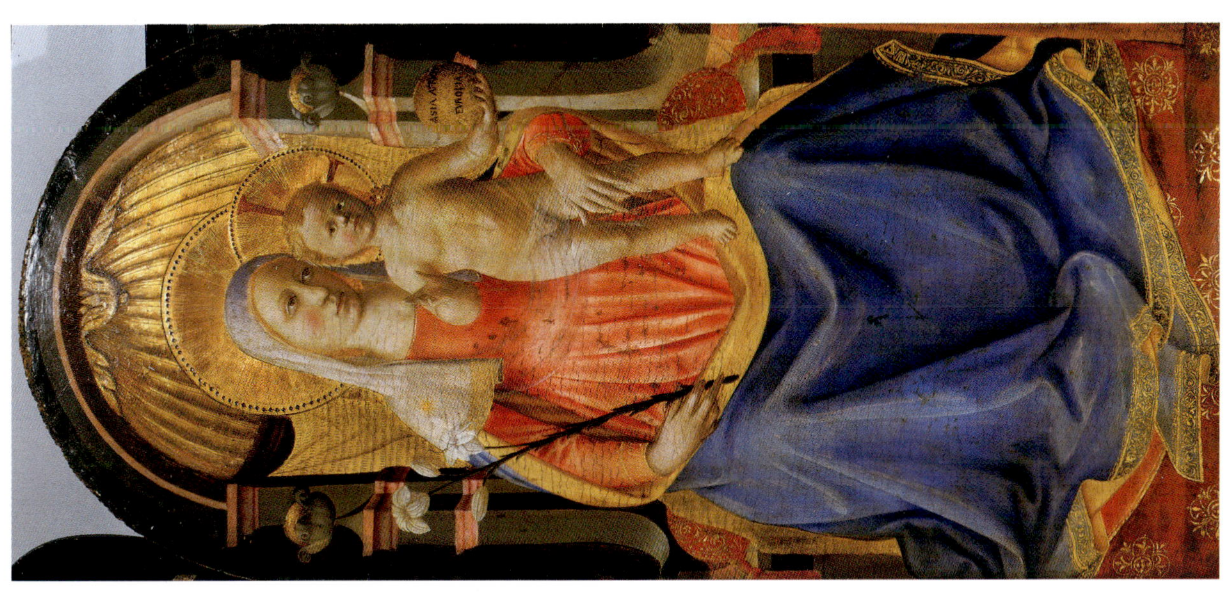

Madonna and Child

Master of the Buckingham Palace Madonna
(Italian, active mid-fifteenth century)
Madonna and Child Enthroned, 1460–1465
Tempera on panel, 89 x 42 cm ($35\frac{1}{16}$ x $16\frac{9}{16}$ in.)
The State Hermitage Museum, St. Petersburg

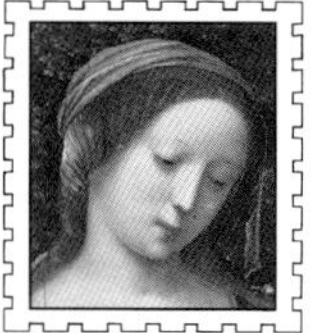

Pomegranate 707 782 9000 WWW.POMEGRANATE.COM

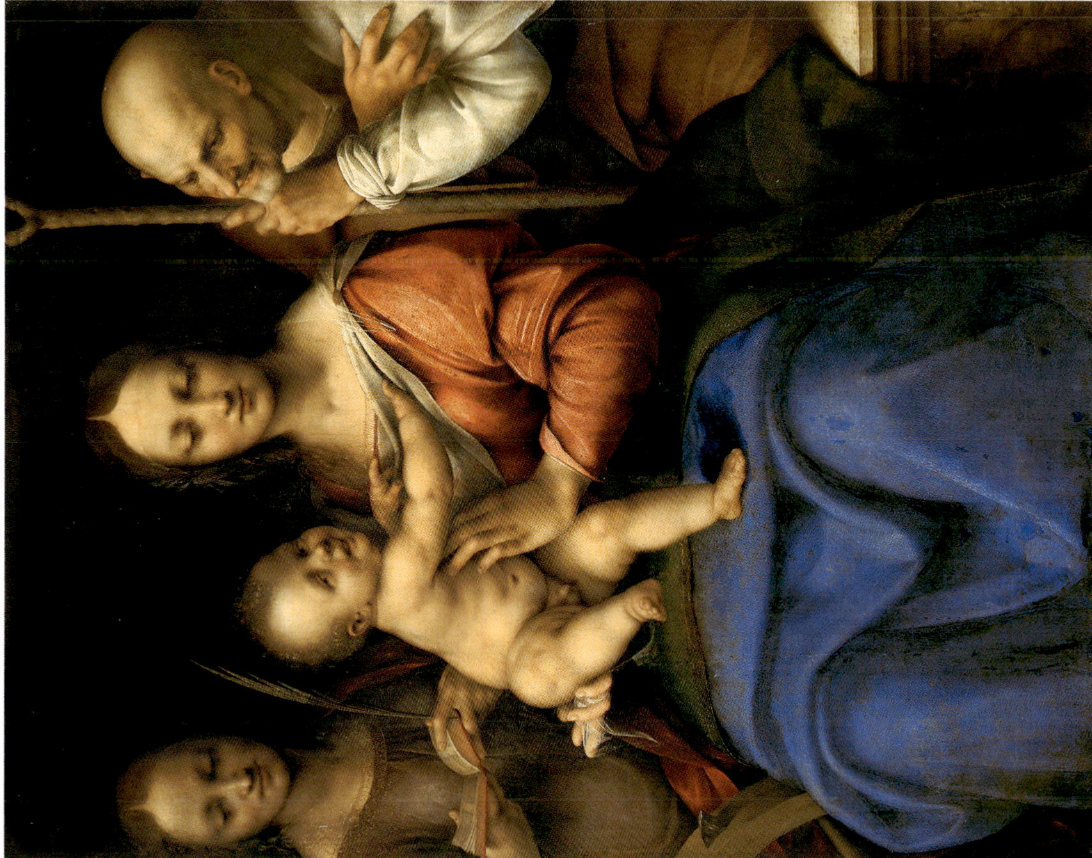

Madonna and Child

Cesare da Sesto (Italian, 1477–1523)
The Holy Family with St. Catherine, 1515–1520
Oil on canvas (transferred from panel),
89 x 71 cm (35 1/16 x 27 15/16 in.)
The State Hermitage Museum, St. Petersburg

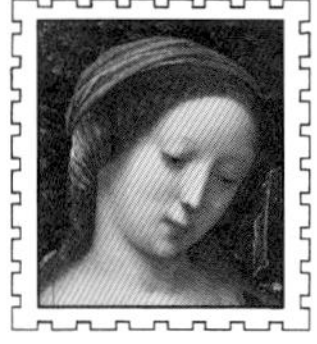

Pomegranate 707 782 9000 WWW.POMEGRANATE.COM

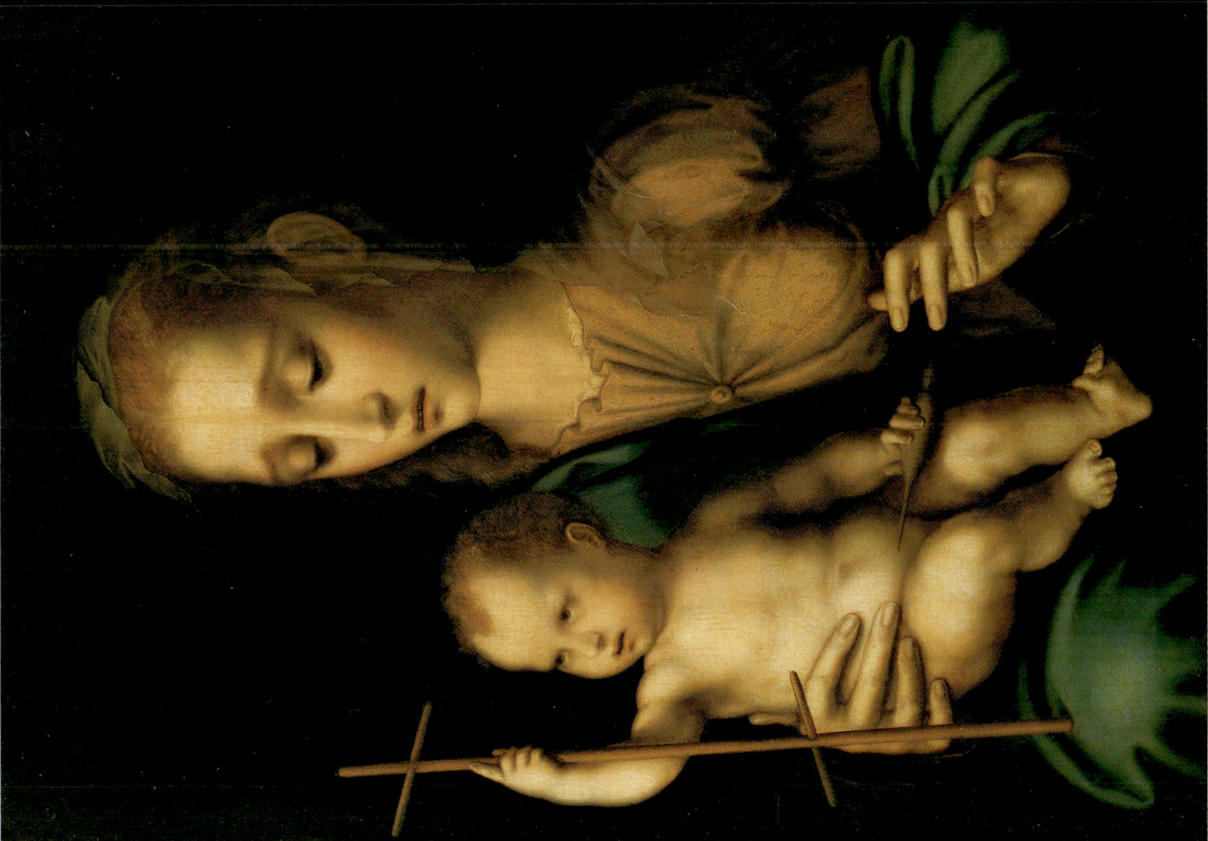

Madonna and Child

Luis de Morales (Spanish, 1509/1519–1585)
The Virgin and Child with a Cross-Shaped Distaff, 1570s
Oil on canvas (transferred from panel),
71.5 x 52 cm (28⅛ x 20½ in.)
The State Hermitage Museum, St. Petersburg

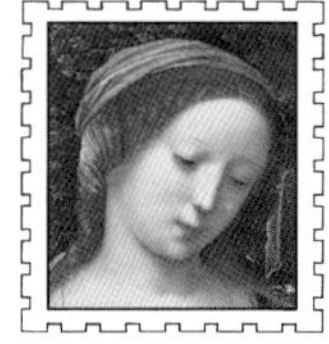

Pomegranate 707 782 9000 WWW.POMEGRANATE.COM

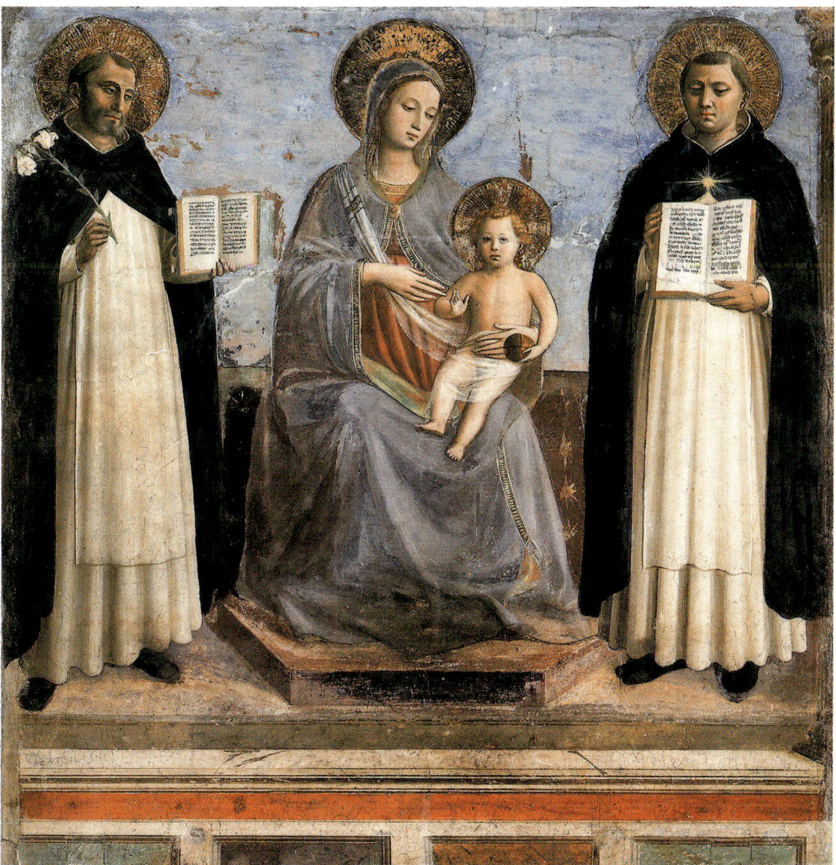

Madonna and Child

Fra Angelico (Fra Giovanni da Fiesole)
(Italian, c. 1395–1455)
Madonna and Child with St. Dominic and St. Thomas Aquinas, 1424–1430
Fresco, 196 x 187 cm (77 9/16 x 73 5/8 in.)
The State Hermitage Museum, St. Petersburg

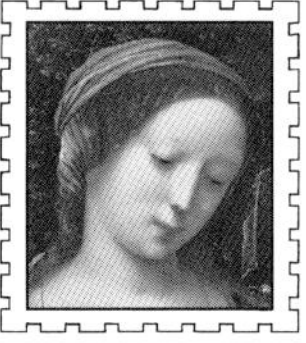

Pomegranate 707 782 9000 WWW.POMEGRANATE.COM

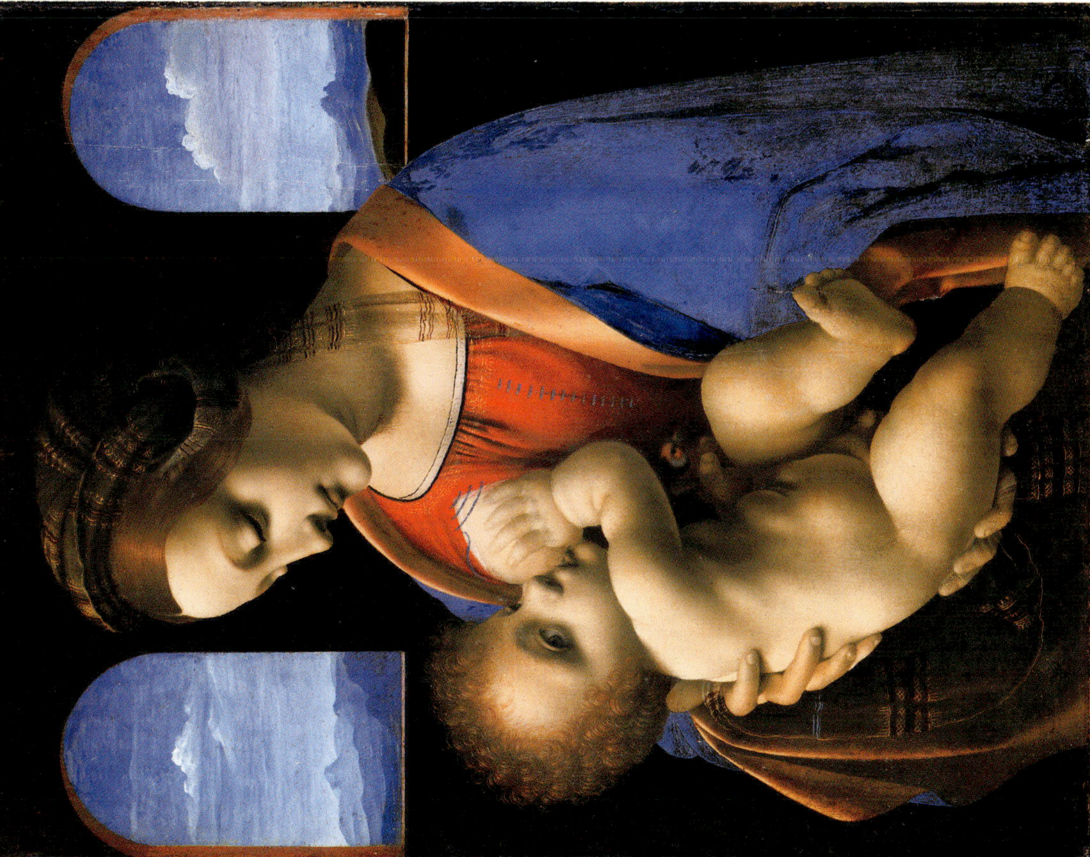

Madonna and Child

Leonardo da Vinci (Italian, 1452–1519)
Madonna and Child (Madonna Litta), 1490–1491
Tempera on canvas (transferred from panel),
42 x 33 cm (16$\frac{9}{16}$ x 13 in.)
The State Hermitage Museum, St. Petersburg

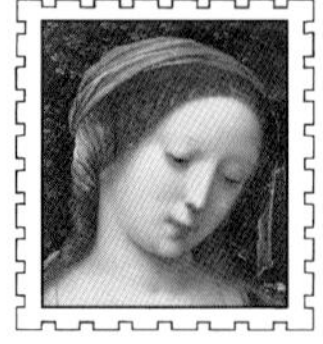

Pomegranate 707 782 9000 WWW.POMEGRANATE.COM

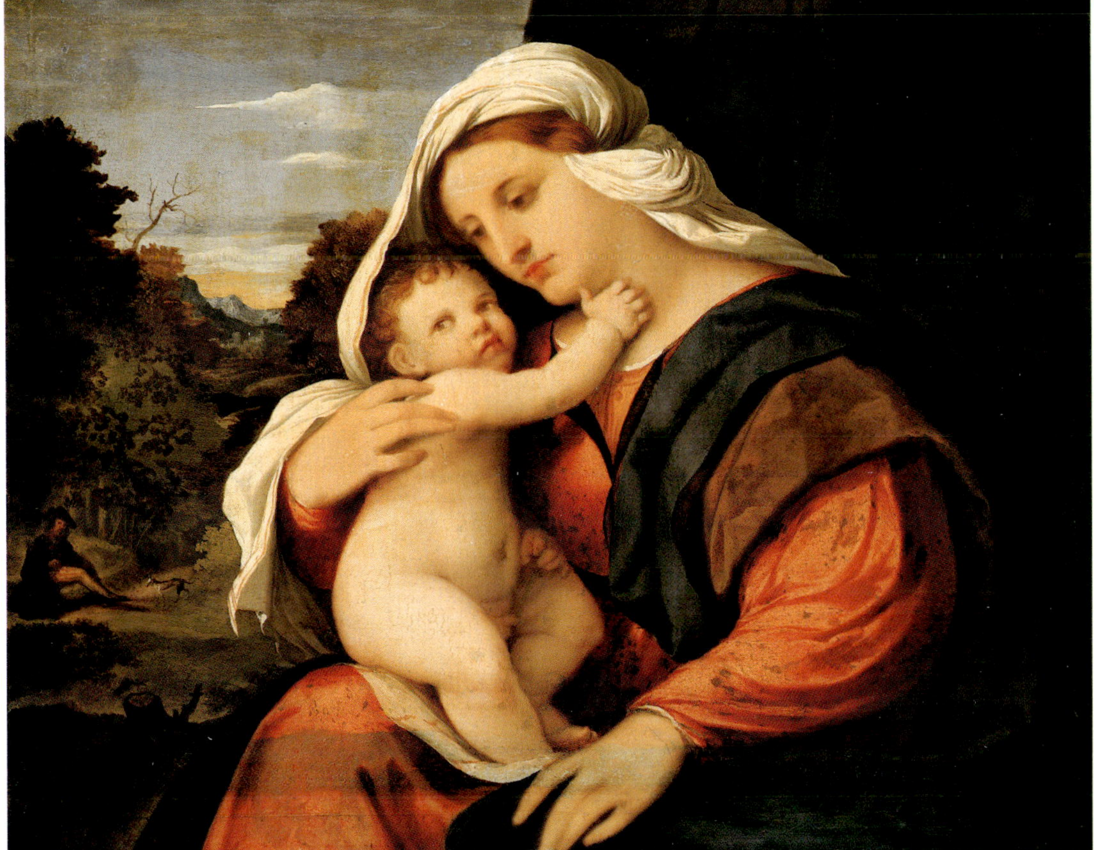

Madonna and Child

Palma il Vecchio (Jacopo Negretti) (Italian, 1480–1528)
Madonna and Child, 1515–1516
Oil on canvas, 59 x 72 cm (23¼ x 28⅜ in.)
The State Hermitage Museum, St. Petersburg

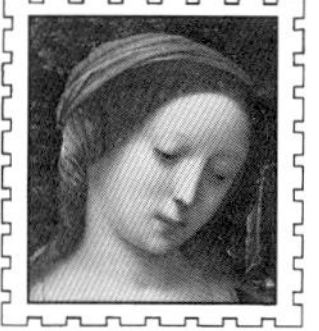

Pomegranate
707 782 9000 WWW.POMEGRANATE.COM

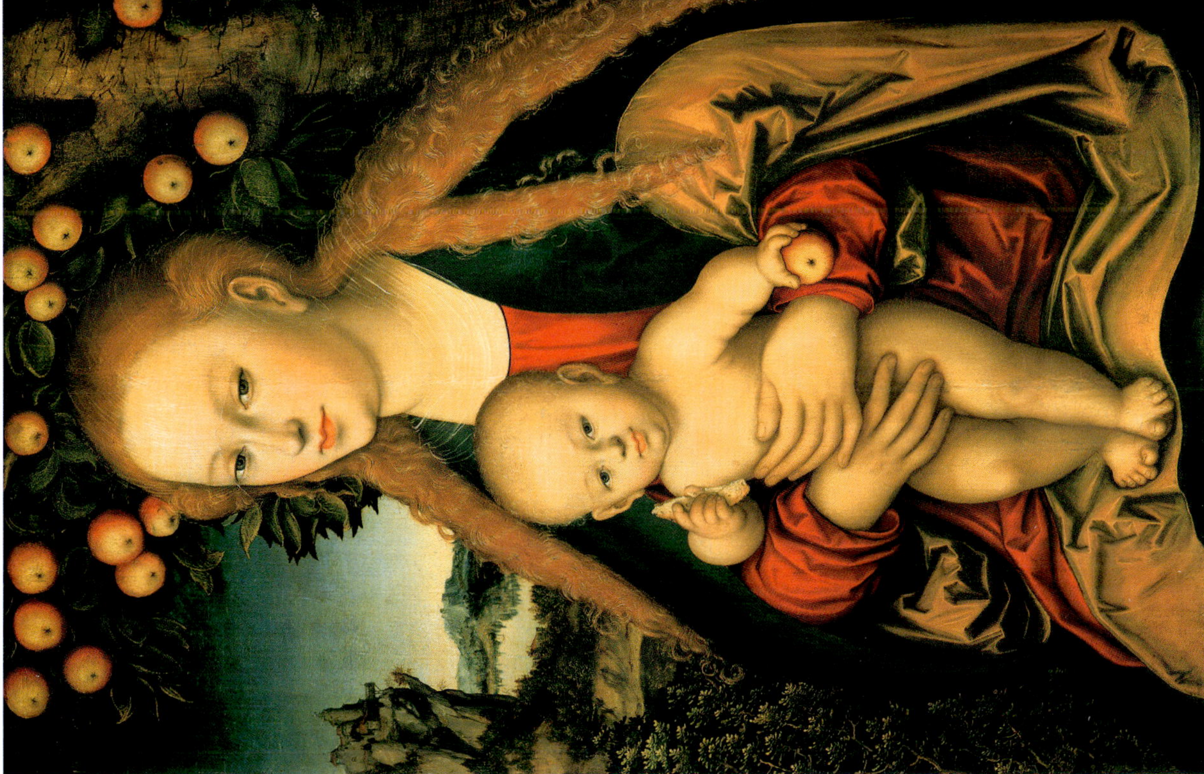

Madonna and Child

Lucas Cranach the Elder (German, 1472–1553)
The Virgin and Child under an Apple Tree, c. 1530
Oil on canvas (transferred from panel),
87 x 59 cm (34¼ x 23¼ in.)
The State Hermitage Museum, St. Petersburg

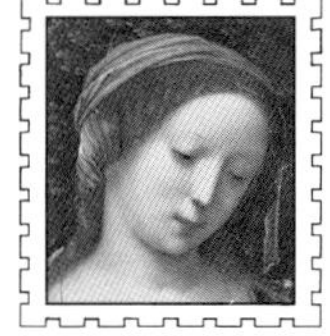

Pomegranate 707 782 9000 WWW.POMEGRANATE.COM

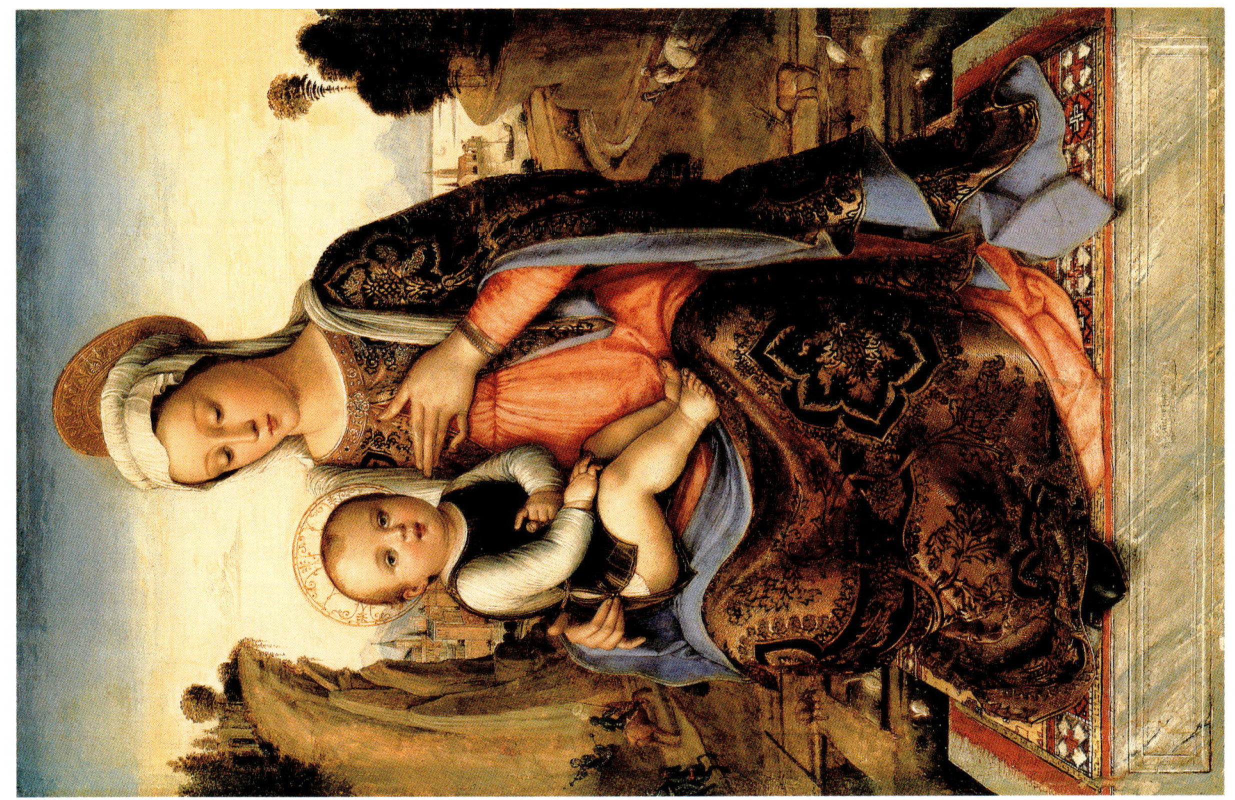

Madonna and Child

Lazzaro Bastiani (Italian, c. 1425–1512)
Madonna and Child, 1480s–1490s
Oil on canvas (transferred from panel),
58 x 38 cm ($22\frac{13}{16}$ x $14\frac{15}{16}$ in.)
The State Hermitage Museum, St. Petersburg

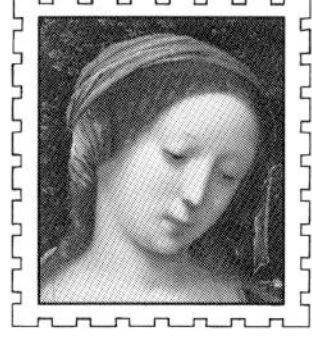

WWW.POMEGRANATE.COM 707 782 9000

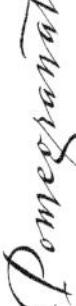

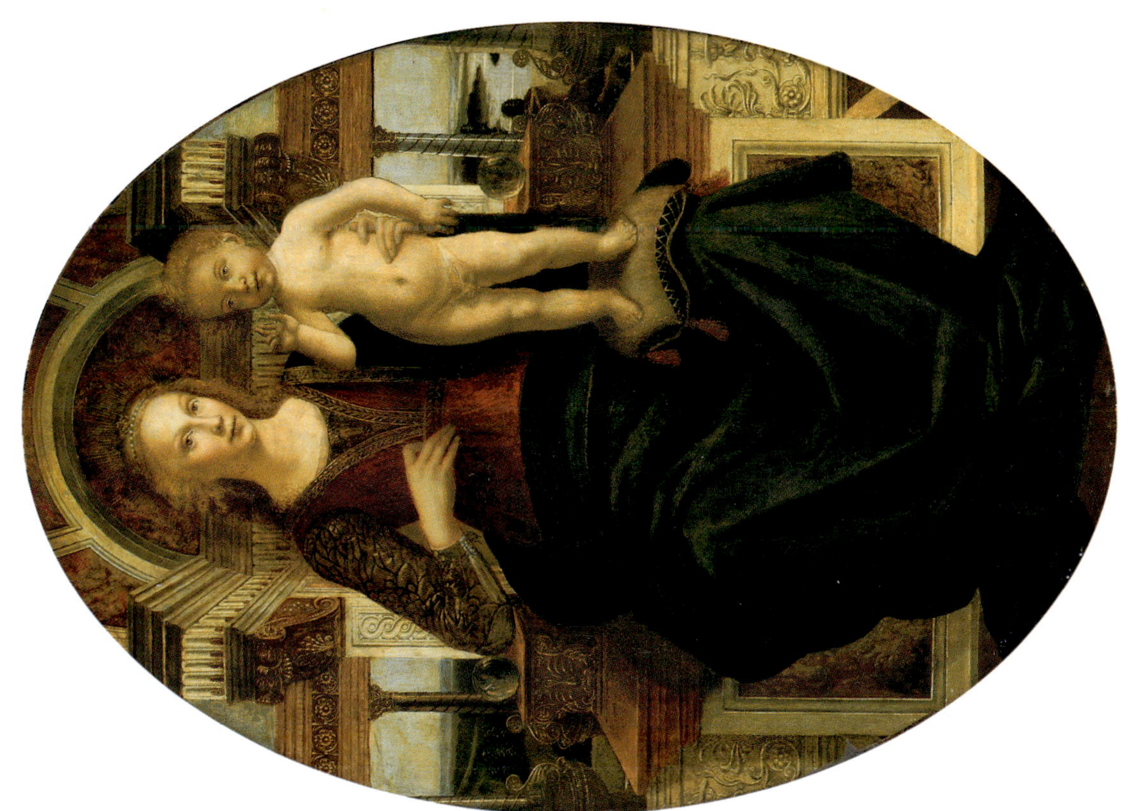

Madonna and Child

School of Andrea del Verrocchio (Italian, c. 1435–1488)
Madonna and Child, late fifteenth century
Tempera and oil on canvas (transferred from panel),
75 x 54 cm (29½ x 21¼ in.)
The State Hermitage Museum, St. Petersburg

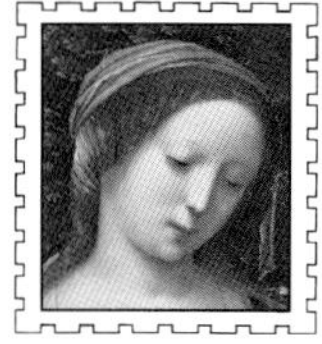

Pomegranate 707 782 9000 WWW.POMEGRANATE.COM

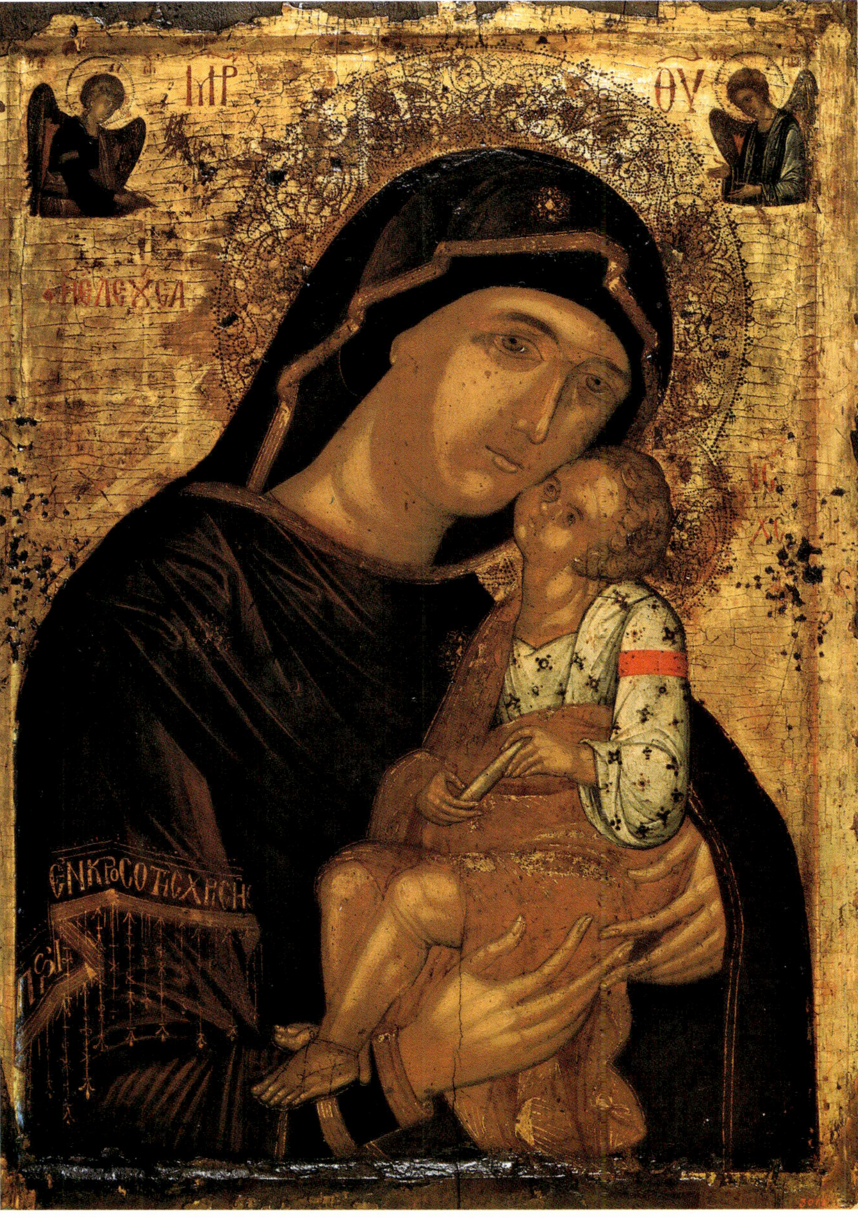
ΜΡ ΘΥ

Madonna and Child

Unknown Byzantine painter
Icon: The Virgin Eleouse, early to mid-fifteenth century
Tempera on panel, 66.2 x 48 cm ($26\frac{1}{16}$ x $18\frac{7}{8}$ in.)
The State Hermitage Museum, St. Petersburg

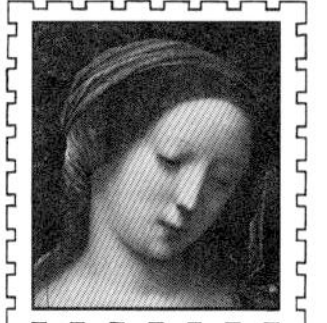

Pomegranate 707 782 9000 WWW.POMEGRANATE.COM

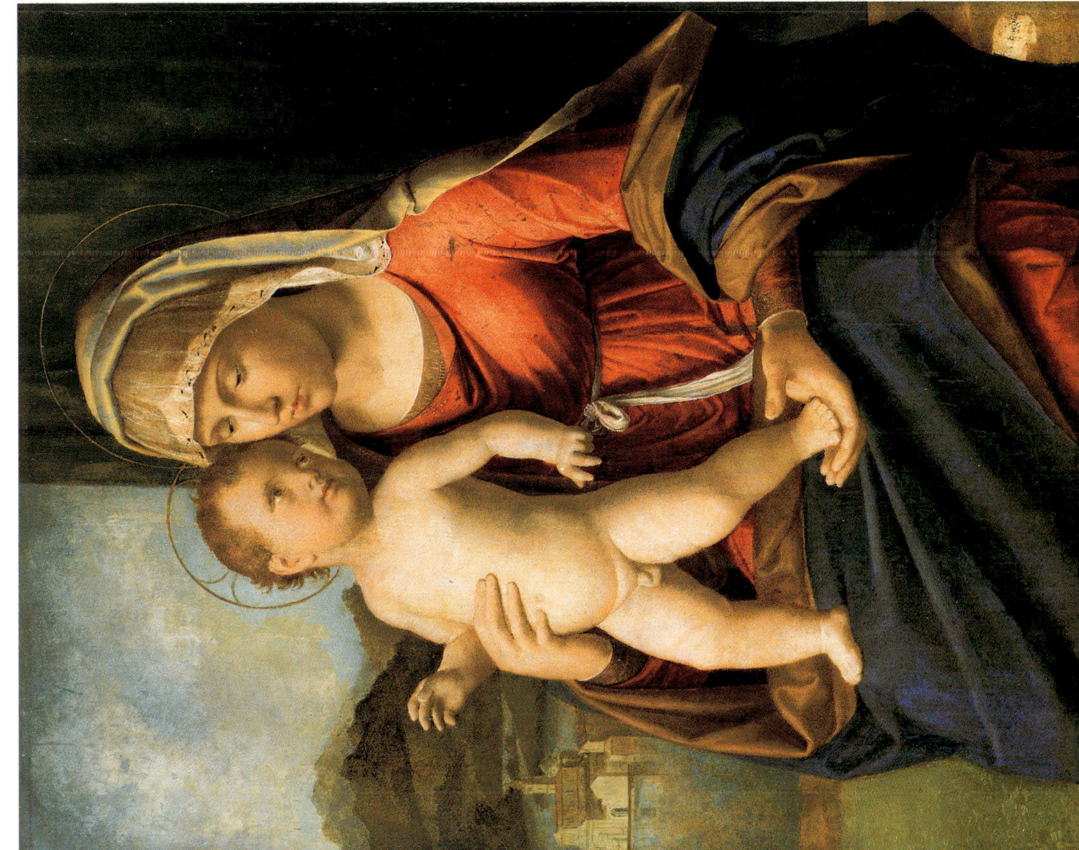

Madonna and Child

Giovanni Battista Cima da Conegliano
(Italian, c. 1459–c. 1517)
Madonna and Child, 1496–1499
Oil on canvas, 65 x 53 cm (25 9/16 x 20 7/8 in.)
The State Hermitage Museum, St. Petersburg

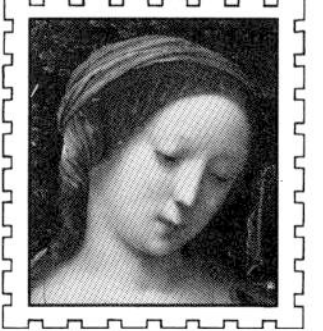

Pomegranate
707 782 9000 WWW.POMEGRANATE.COM

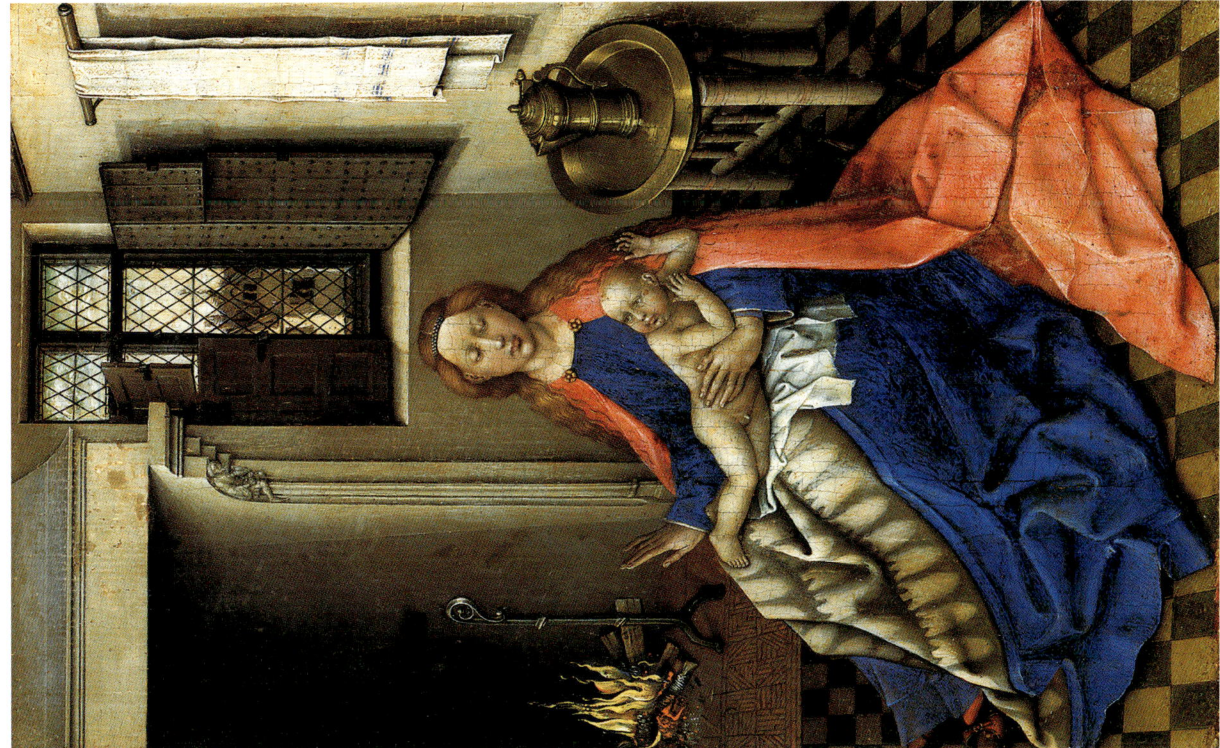

Madonna and Child

Robert Campin (Master of Flémalle)
(Netherlandish, c. 1380–1444)
The Virgin and Child by a Fireplace
(right wing of a diptych), c. 1433–1435
Oil on panel, 34.3 x 24.5 cm (13½ x 9⅝ in.)
The State Hermitage Museum, St. Petersburg

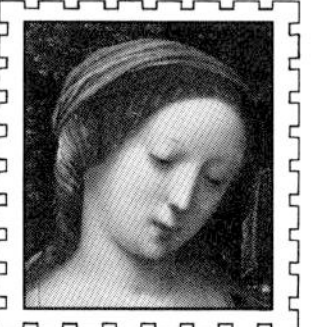

Pomegranate 707 782 9000 WWW.POMEGRANATE.COM

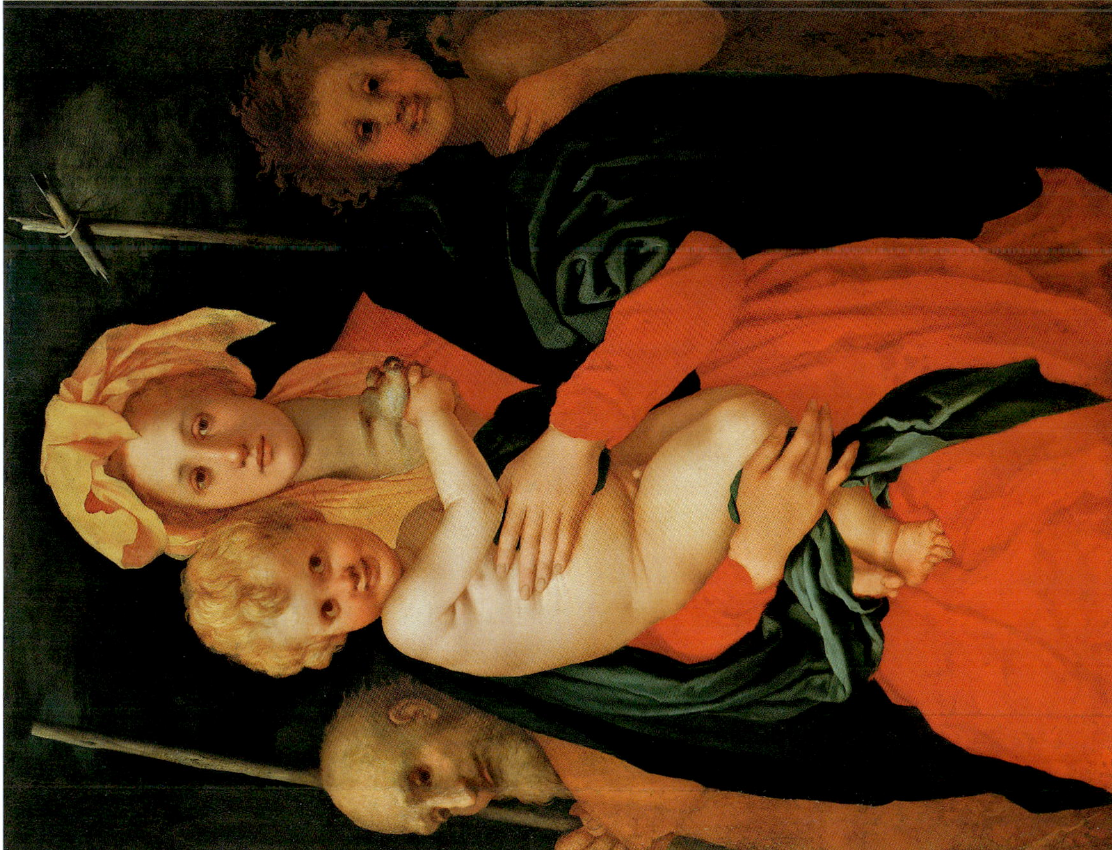

Madonna and Child

Pontormo (Jacopo Carrucci) (Italian, 1494–1557)
Madonna and Child with St. Joseph and St. John the Baptist, 1521–1522
Oil on canvas, 120 x 98.5 cm (47¼ x 38¾ in.)
The State Hermitage Museum, St. Petersburg

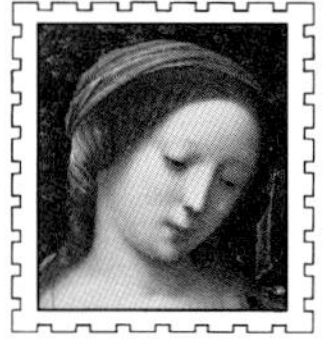

Pomegranate
707 782 9000 WWW.POMEGRANATE.COM

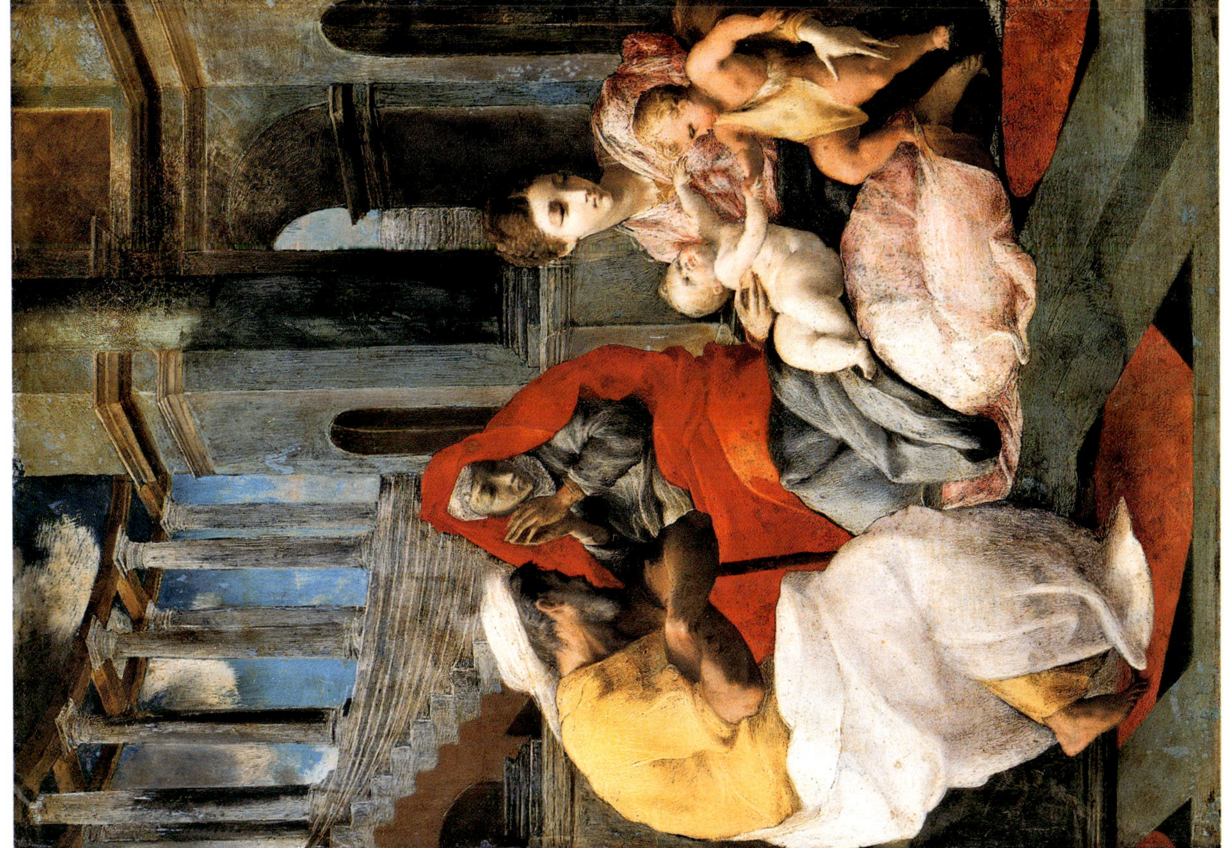

Madonna and Child

Francesco Primaticcio (Italian, 1504–1570)
The Holy Family with St. Elizabeth and St. John the Baptist, 1541–1543
Oil on slate, 43.5 x 31 cm (17 ⅛ x 12 3/16 in.)
The State Hermitage Museum, St. Petersburg

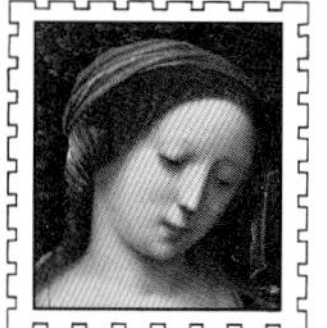

Pomegranate 707 782 9000 WWW.POMEGRANATE.COM

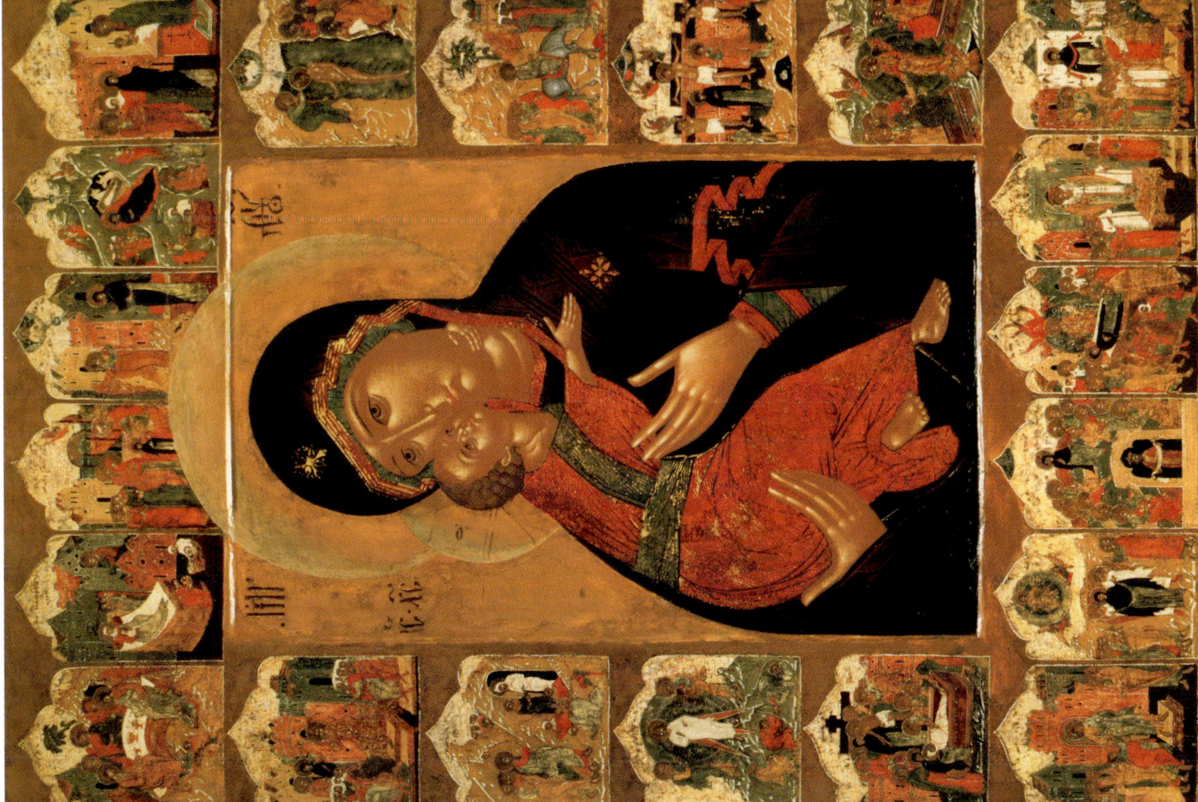

Madonna and Child

Unknown Russian painter
Icon: The Virgin of Vladimir with Church Feasts,
early seventeenth century
Tempera on panel, 103 x 71 cm (40 9/16 x 27 15/16 in.)
The State Hermitage Museum, St. Petersburg

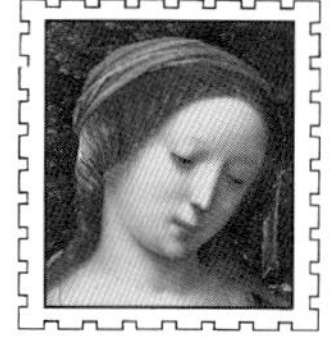

Pomegranate 707 782 9000 WWW.POMEGRANATE.COM

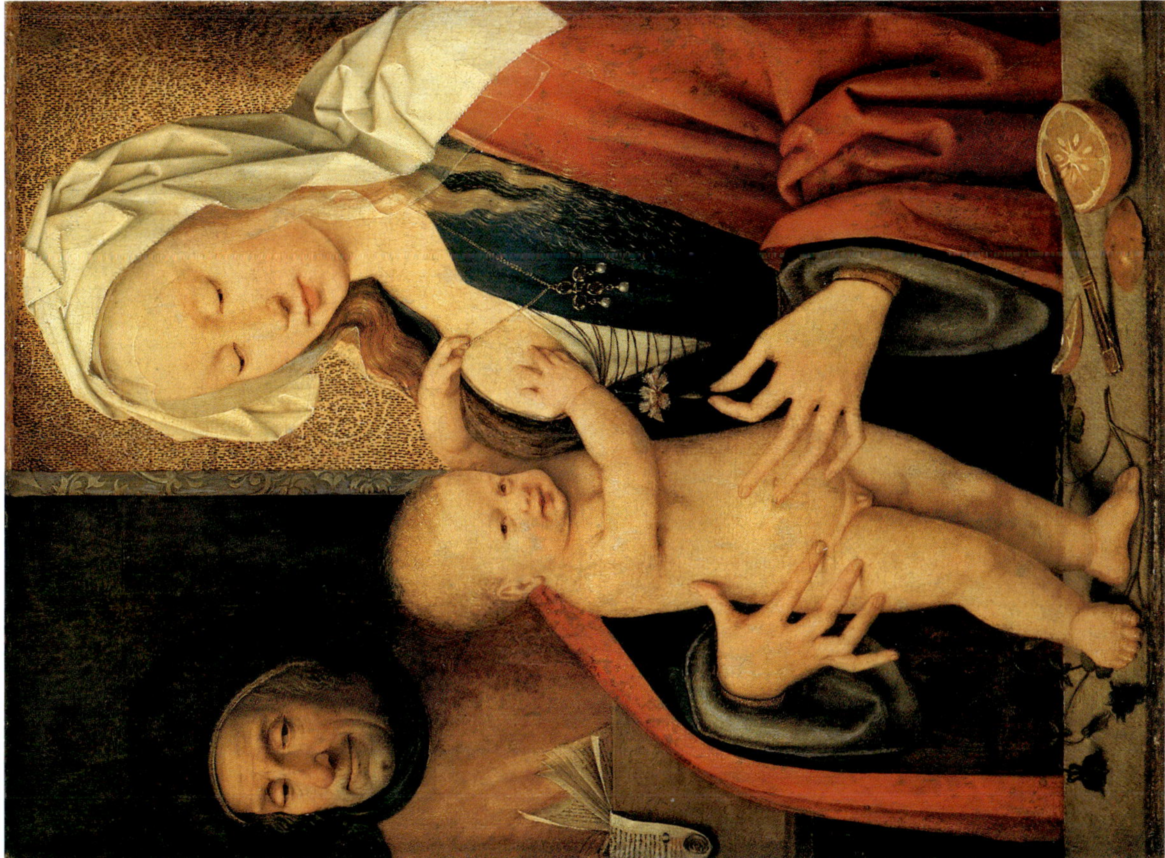

Madonna and Child

Joos van Cleve (Netherlandish, 1464–c. 1540)
The Holy Family, n.d.
Oil on canvas (transferred from panel),
42.5 x 31.5 cm (16¾ x 12⅜ in.)
The State Hermitage Museum, St. Petersburg

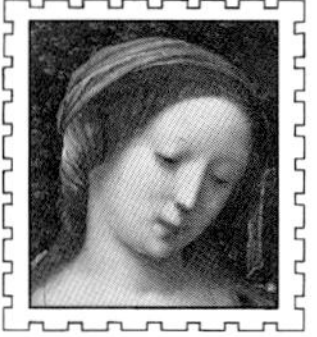

Pomegranate 707 782 9000 WWW.POMEGRANATE.COM

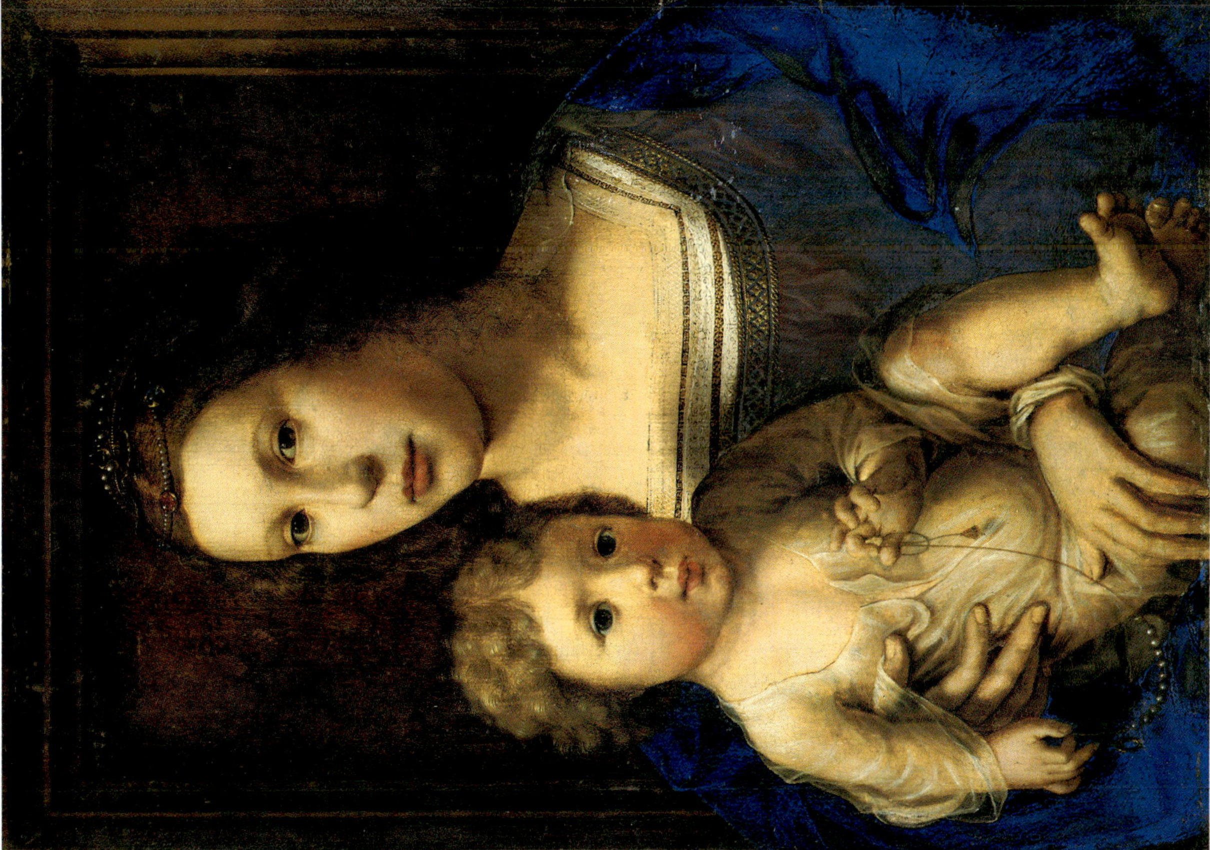

Madonna and Child

Jan Gossaert (called Mabuse) (Netherlandish, 1478–1532)
The Virgin and Child (sixteenth-century copy)
Oil on panel, 44 x 32.2 cm (17 5/16 x 12 11/16 in.)
The State Hermitage Museum, St. Petersburg

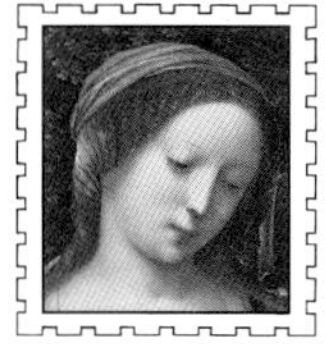

Pomegranate
707 782 9000 WWW.POMEGRANATE.COM

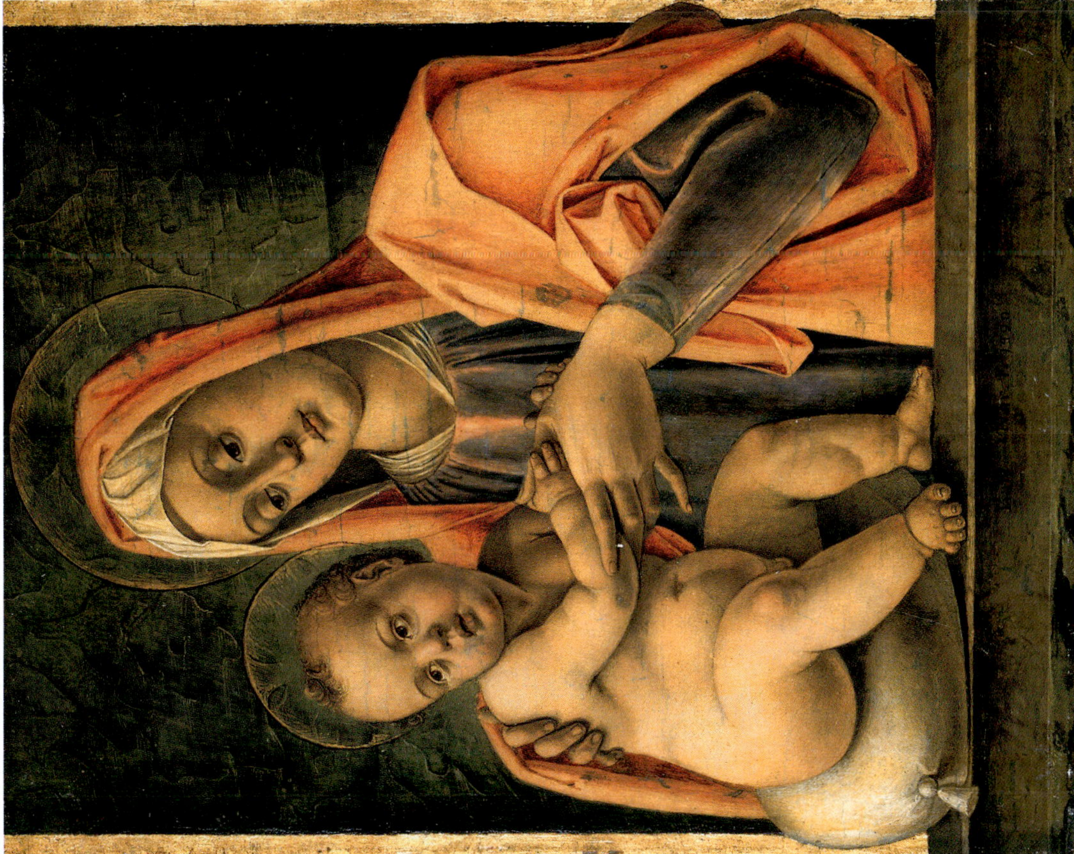

Madonna and Child

Bartolomeo Vivarini (Italian, c. 1432–after 1491)
Madonna and Child, 1490
Tempera on canvas (transferred from panel),
57.5 x 46.5 cm (22⅝ x 18 5⁄16 in.)
The State Hermitage Museum, St. Petersburg

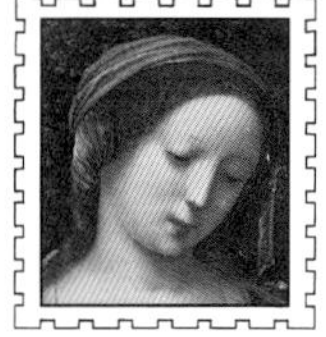

Pomegranate 707 782 9000 WWW.POMEGRANATE.COM

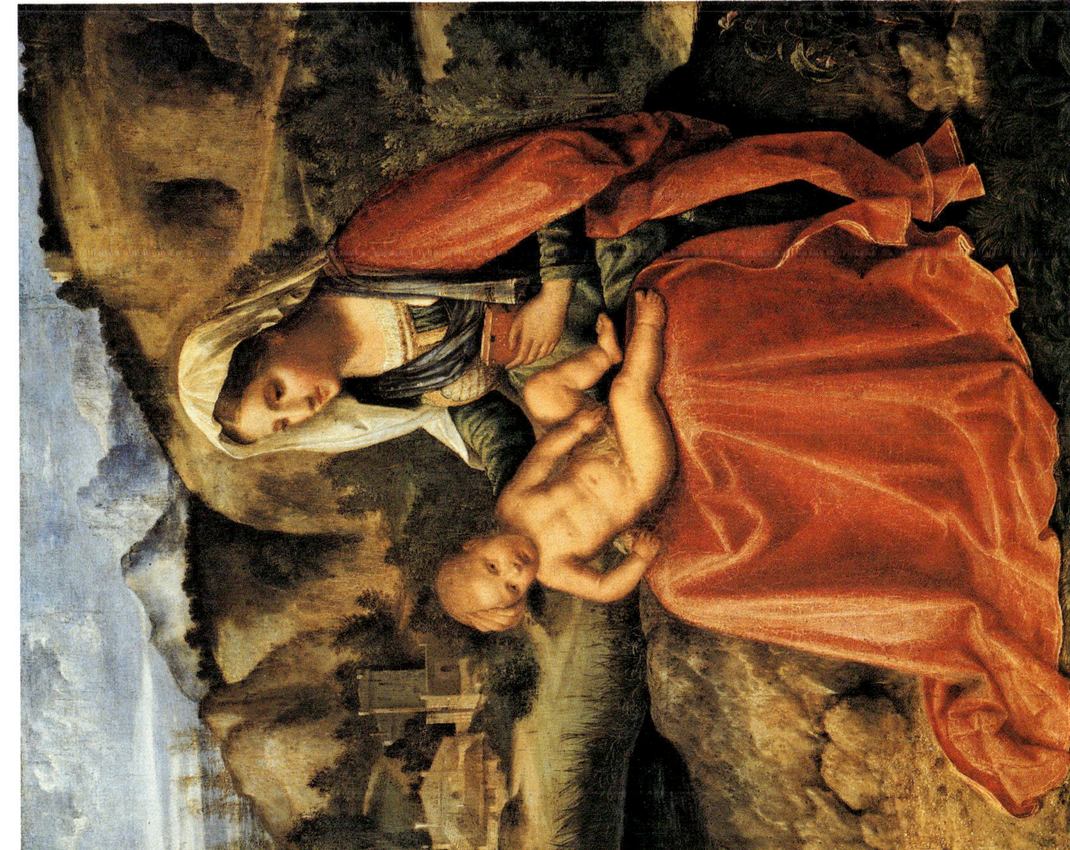

Madonna and Child

Giorgione (Giorgio da Castelfranco) (Italian, c. 1478–1510)
Madonna and Child in a Landscape, c. 1503
Oil on canvas (transferred from panel),
44 x 36.5 cm (17⁵⁄₁₆ x 14⅜ in.)
The State Hermitage Museum, St. Petersburg

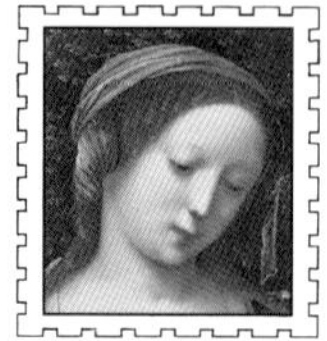

Pomegranate 707 782 9000 WWW.POMEGRANATE.COM

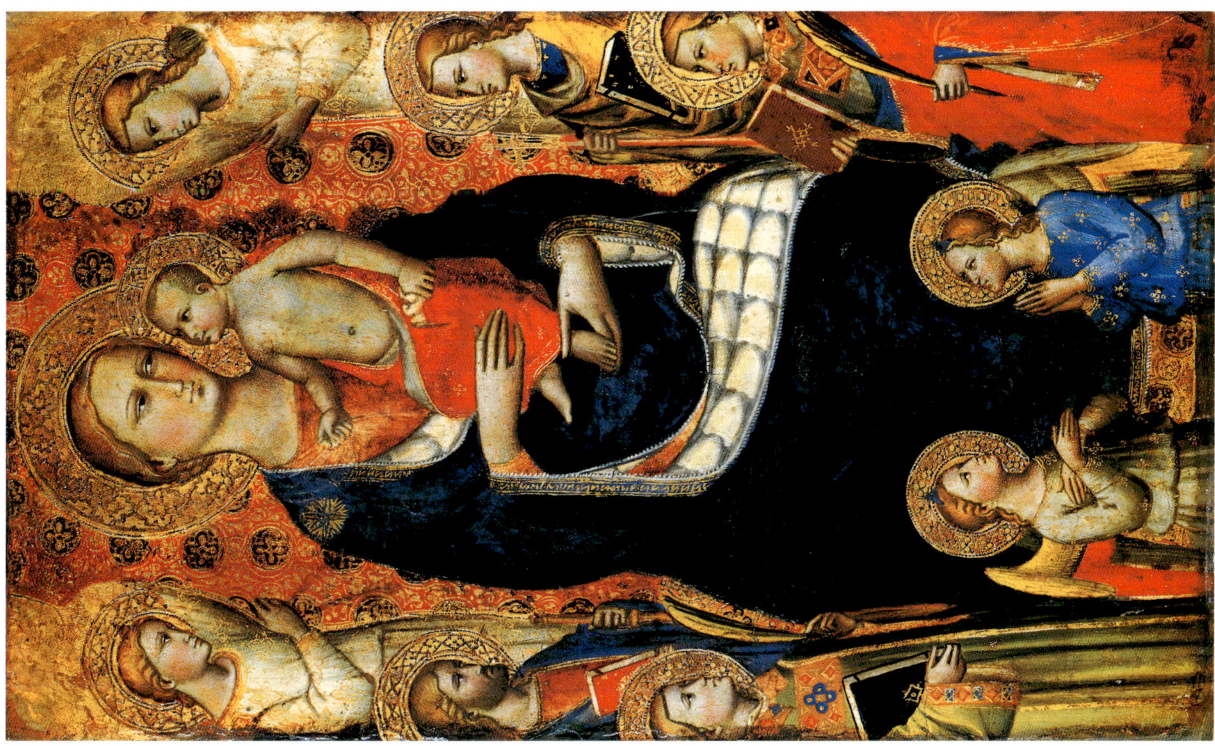

Madonna and Child

Master of the Arte della Lana
(Italian, active late fourteenth–early fifteenth centuries)
Madonna and Child with Four Saints and Four Angels, n.d.
Tempera on panel, 62.5 x 37 cm (24⅝ x 14⁹⁄₁₆ in.)
The State Hermitage Museum, St. Petersburg

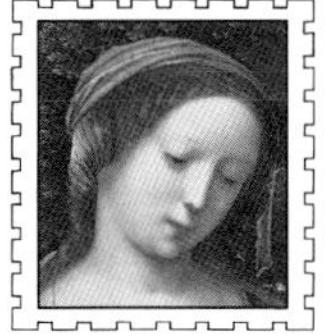

Pomegranate 707 782 9000 WWW.POMEGRANATE.COM

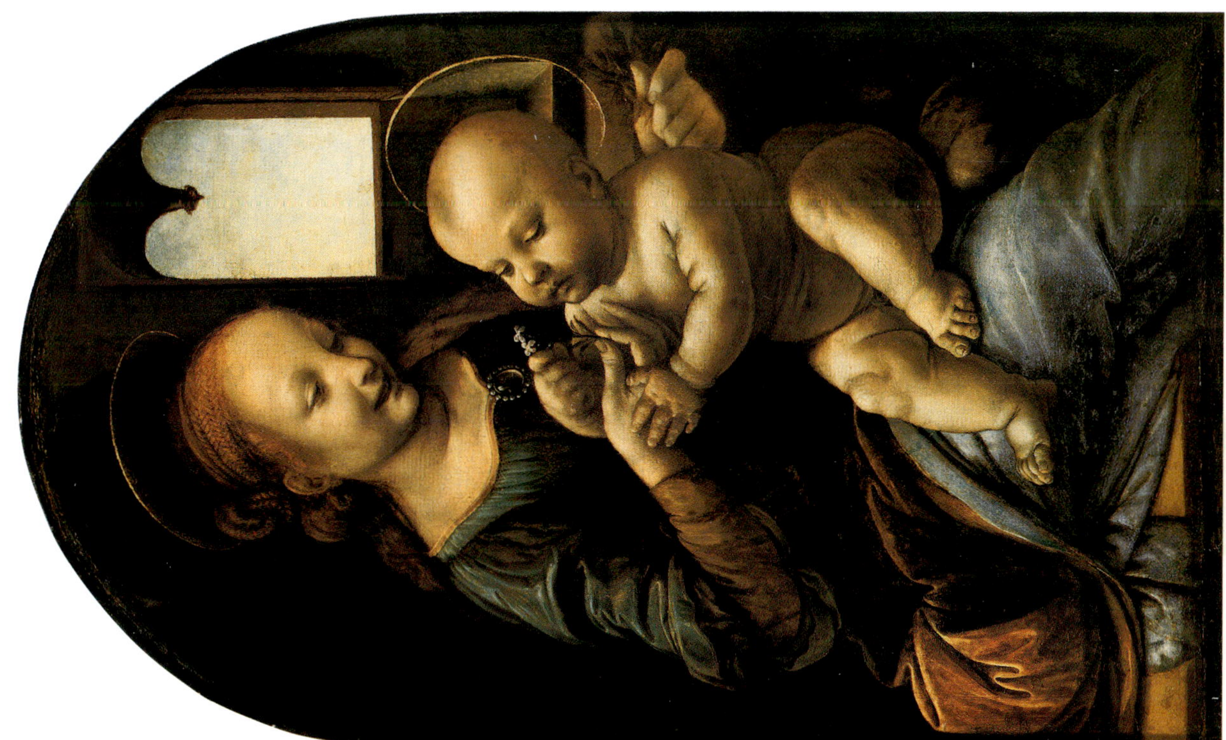

Madonna and Child

Leonardo da Vinci (Italian, 1452–1519)
Madonna with a Flower (The Benois Madonna), 1478–1480
Oil on canvas (transferred from panel),
49.5 x 33 cm (19½ x 13 in.)
The State Hermitage Museum, St. Petersburg

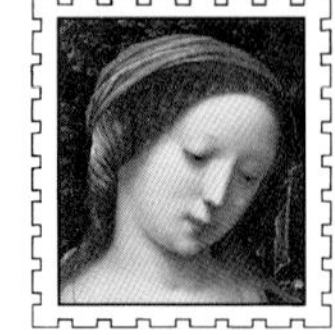

Pomegranate 707 782 9000 WWW.POMEGRANATE.COM

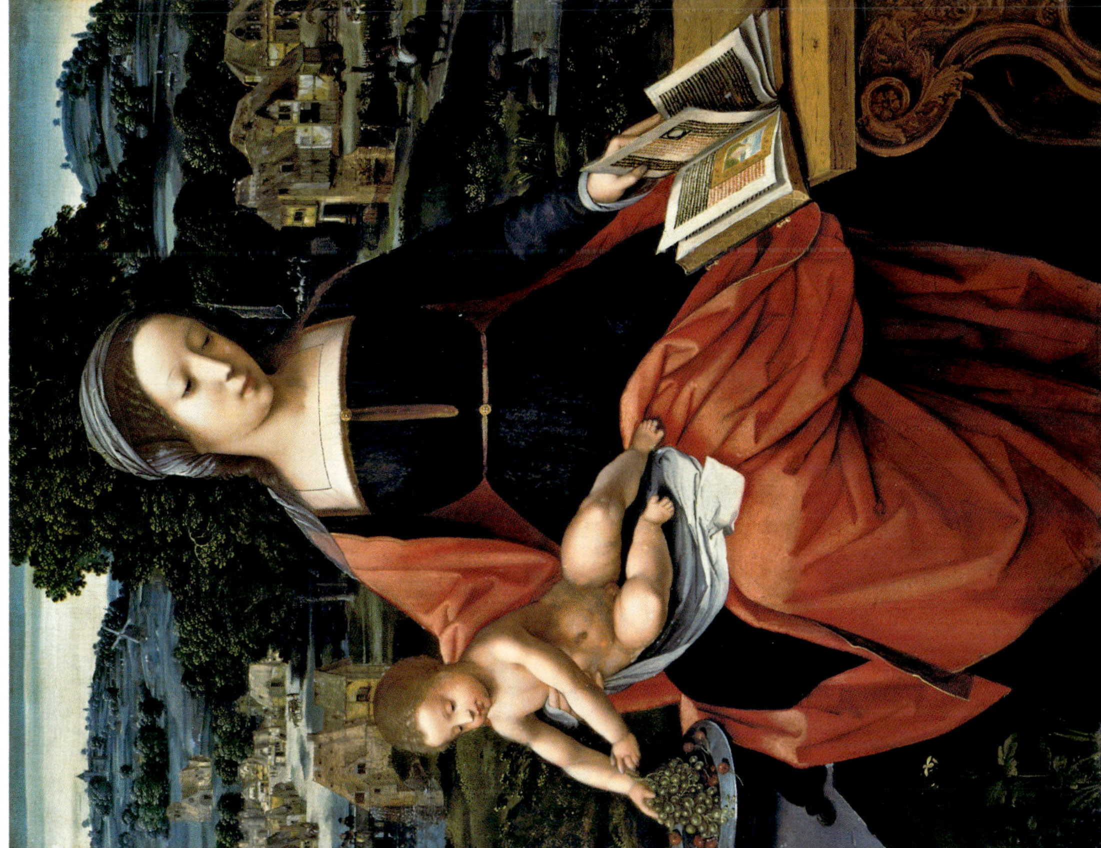

Madonna and Child

Master of the Female Half-Lengths
(Netherlandish, active first half of the sixteenth century)
The Virgin and Child, n.d.
Oil on panel, 53.2 x 42.4 cm ($20\frac{15}{16}$ x $16\frac{11}{16}$ in.)
The State Hermitage Museum, St. Petersburg

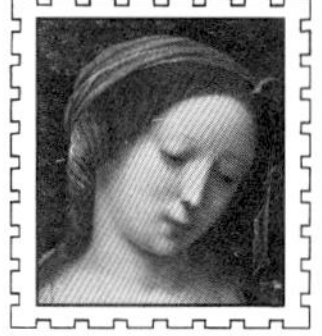

Pomegranate 707 782 9000 WWW.POMEGRANATE.COM

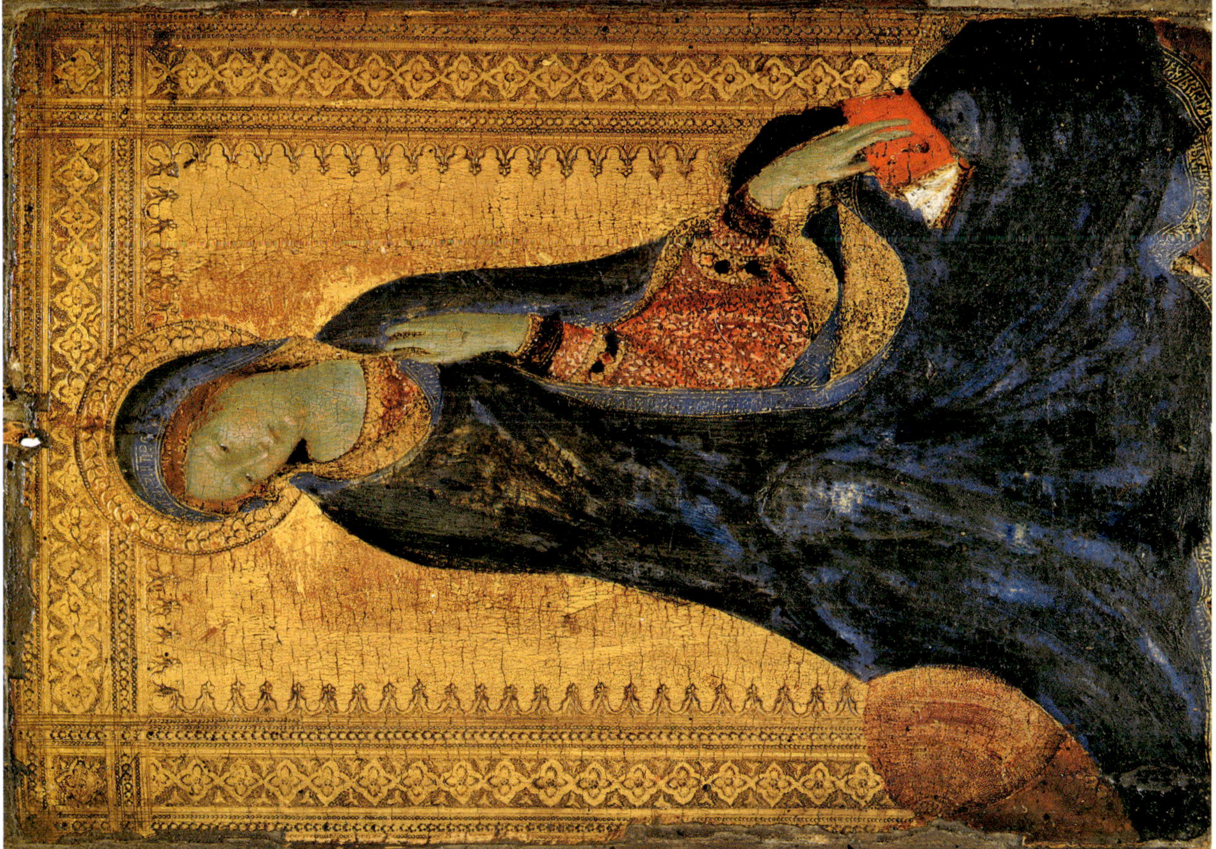

Madonna and Child

Simone Martini (Italian, c. 1284–1344)
The Virgin Annunciate, 1340–1344
Tempera on panel, 30.5 x 21.5 cm (12 x 8 7⁄16 in.)
The State Hermitage Museum, St. Petersburg

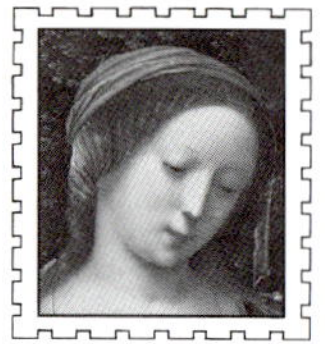

Pomegranate 707 782 9000 WWW.POMEGRANATE.COM

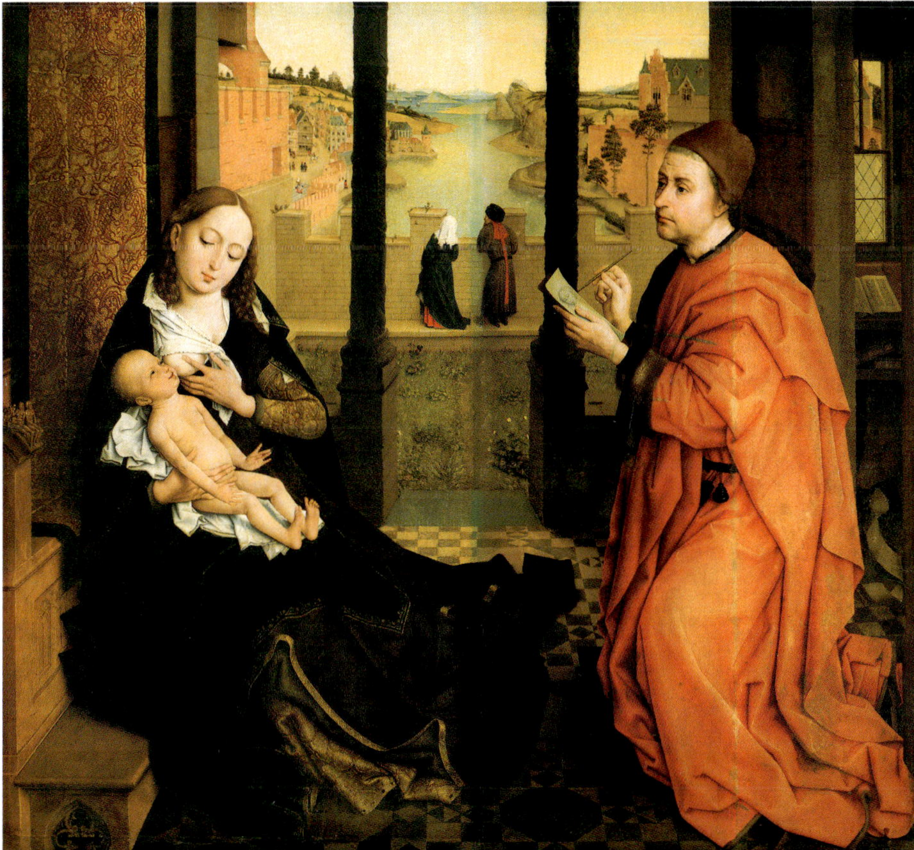

Madonna and Child

Rogier van der Weyden (Netherlandish, c. 1400–1464)
St. Luke Drawing the Virgin, n.d.
Oil on canvas (transferred from panel),
102.5 x 108.5 cm (40⅜ x 42 11/16 in.)
The State Hermitage Museum, St. Petersburg

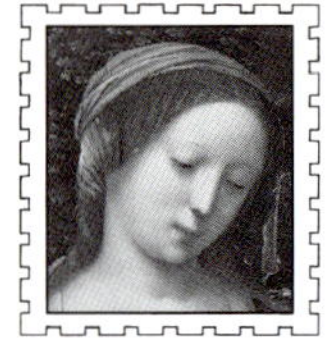

Pomegranate 707 782 9000 WWW.POMEGRANATE.COM

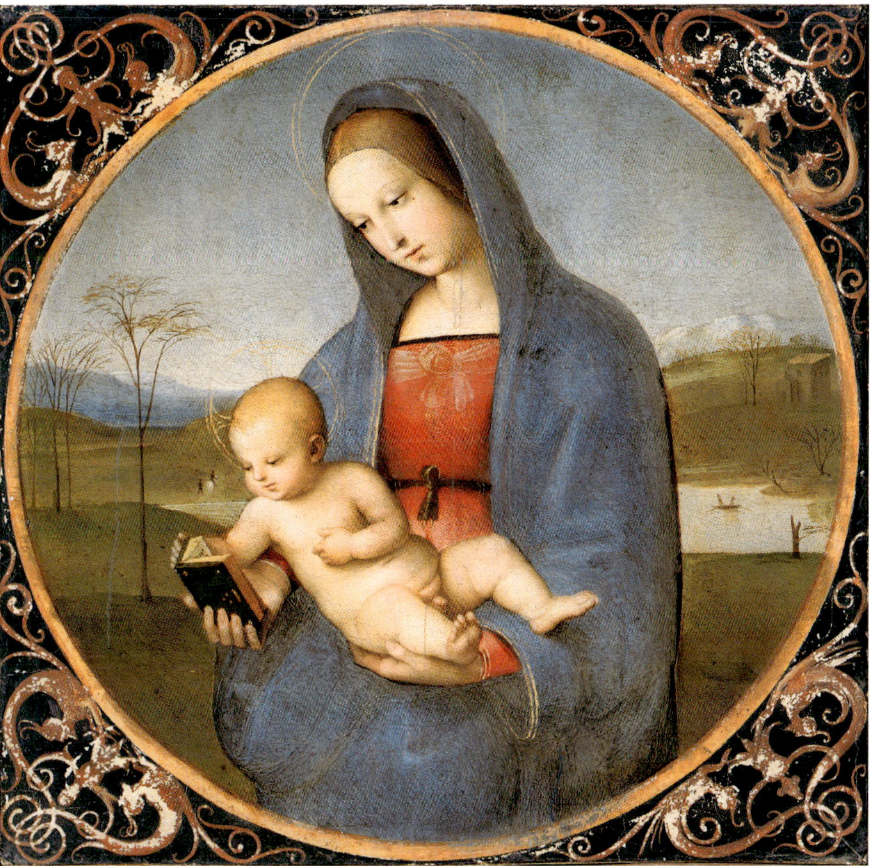

Madonna and Child

Raphael (Raffaello Santi or Sanzio) (Italian, 1483–1520)
Madonna and Child (Madonna Conestabile), c. 1504
Tempera on canvas (transferred from panel),
17.5 x 18 cm (6⅞ x 7 1⁄16 in.)
The State Hermitage Museum, St. Petersburg

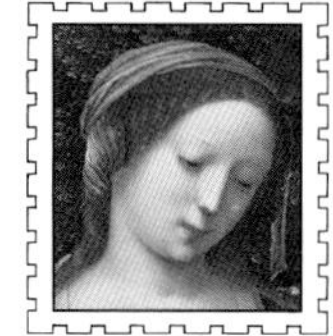

Pomegranate 707 782 9000 WWW.POMEGRANATE.COM